SOUTH KELSEY

The History of a North Lincolnshire Village

by

Jean Collins

UP

U P Publications
2009

First published in Great Britain in 2009 by

U P Publications Ltd

Eco Innovation Centre, PetersCourt, City Road, Peterborough PE1 2SA

Cover design copyright © G. M. Griffin Peers 2009

Cover Map Detail from an "Antique Map of Lincolnshire" it is a "royalty-free stock image for all purposes with no usage credit required" http://www.fromoldbooks.org

Other photographs used on the Cover and within the text are reproduced here by Jean Collins with the permission of their owners.

Copyright © Jean Collins 2008

Jean Collins has asserted her moral rights

A CIP Catalogue record of this book is available from the British Library

ISBN 978-0-9557447-3-0 Paperback

ISBN 978-1-9081357-8-0 eBook

Printed in England by The Lightning Source Group

www.uppbooks.com

CONTENTS

LIST OF CHARTS

LIST OF PLATES

Figs. 1–5   Thatched Cottages from before the War

Fig. 6   The Balderson Family outside their shop on the Crossroads

Fig. 7   Balderson's Bus - The First South Kelsey Bus

Fig. 8   The Kirby's Shop on Brigg Road

Figs. 9-11   The old Forge on Brigg Road in the 1900s, 1920s and 1930s (with the Bicycle Shop on the left of the Bottom Picture).

Figs.12-14   The Village Post Office, Thornton Road.

Fig. 15   Moortown House 1938

Fig. 16   Caistor Road. Methodist Sunday School & School Farm.

Fig. 17   Caistor Road. Sunshine Farmhouse showing the Butcher's Shop on the end wall.

Fig. 18   The Crossroads early 1900s "The Bull Inn" - note thatched roof. The cottage on the right belonged to the Bacon family before it was pulled down.

Fig. 19   Caistor Road - Looking towards "The Bull Inn"

Fig. 20   Pupils lining the railings of the Village School.

Fig. 21   Manor Farm c. 1900 with ladies from the Green family.

Fig. 22   Hall Farm viewed across the Moat.

Fig. 23   A nineteenth century funeral bier.

Fig. 24   The Mortuary Chapel in the graveyard of St. Nicholas Church – it was demolished in the 1980s.

Figs. 25-27   Old pre-War photos of the Old Rectory also known as the Old Vicarage. The building was destroyed during the Second World War.

Fig. 28   A Post-war photograph of St. Mary's Church showing the original pinnacles on the tower, taken down in 1987 for safety reasons.

Fig. 29   The Thirteenth Century tomb of Sir Robert Hansard.

Fig. 30   A sketch of the Tudor Hall by local artist, Tom Robinson, based on contemporary descriptions.

FOREWORD

I was first tempted to explore the history of South Kelsey when the Church had a flower festival in the Millennium Year and I offered to type out the leaflet describing St. Mary's Church. As a newcomer to the village I knew very little of its history or its people, but as I investigated further it seemed there had to be many stories tucked away in a community that had existed here for at least a thousand years.

Having no formal training as a historian, I set about looking for books of local interest and, dipping into the many available in the local libraries, I gradually started to form a composite picture of how the village must have developed over the centuries. Occasionally I found specific mention of South Kelsey but where I could find no particular reference to the village and to maintain the continuity of the narrative I have outlined the events taking place in the surrounding area which would have made their impact. Of particular help were some of the books by T. W. Beastall, R. J. Olney and Rex Russell.

During my research I met members of the Industrial Archaeology Society who shared their knowledge of canals and mills, in particular Chris Padley, whose knowledge of the Caistor Canal has given me a very comprehensive picture of its history. I have studied documents and maps at the Historic Environment Record in Lincoln where they were of great assistance to me and visited the Lincoln History & Archaeology Society in Jews Court. Irwen and Hilary Johnston of Winghale Books have also loaned me numerous books, pamphlets and maps of the area.

Surfing the Internet gave me yet more pieces of the jigsaw. By this means, I got in touch with Mary Skipworth in New Zealand who has been researching her family history for thirty years and has sent me a lot of valuable information

For the history of the families who have lived in the village for the last century or so, I have talked to the villagers themselves and they have shared their memories, recollections and photographs, some of which, with their kind permission, are included in this book.

As the book has progressed rather more ambitiously than I had at first envisaged, I hope to present a coherent account of many of the events and people that make this a history of a typical rural North Lincolnshire village.

Some of the earlier dates quoted are approximate as various sources did not always agree and some of my conclusions are conjectural.

September 2008

EARLY HISTORY

There is no obvious translation of the name Kelsey, but "ey" is probably derived from the Olde English word for island or more precisely a piece of high ground set in marshy ground. Referred to variously as Colesi or Chelsi in the Domesday Book and after, it was not until 1262 the first reference is made to Suth Kellrseye.

The Anglo-Saxon farmers were fond of the lush pastures obtained by draining swamp land and built their houses on 'Eys - dry islands above the marshes. This would describe the village's location on rising ground in the low lying valley of the Ancholme which, until the New Ancholme was constructed helping to drain the surrounding land, was always liable to flooding. Nearer the river itself, which forms the western boundary of the parish, are the "carrs" - originally meaning marshy ground used for pasturage during the dry season and containing the typical waterside shrubs, like alder and willow.

Around the year 960 AD the Anglo Saxons formed parishes, setting boundaries around the Church, within which the inhabitants would have to pay to the Church the new tax (or "tithe") of $1/10^{th}$ of their annual income.

Between the former marshes of the Ancholme valley and the Wolds were stretches of poor sandy "moorish" grounds covered in gorse, heather and fern and, in times of flood, small lakes and pools. The area was alive with wildfowl, game and vermin of all kinds but much of the land lay uncultivated until the early nineteenth century. Remains of this land were probably contained in the Furze Leas mentioned on an early map, where the villagers would have collected brushwood for their fires.

The Anglo-Saxon settlers liked to form nucleated settlements called "vills" or "tuns" where all the farms and cottages were grouped together possibly within a stockade or similar defence and established the open-field system of farming. This created a countryside with few hedges and trees except perhaps in the "closes" (enclosed fields) near the village The two open fields would have been divided up into hundreds of strips, each strip containing between two and five plough-ridges, the "ridge and furrow" corrugations still visible in one or two of the fields around the village.

The head of each peasant family, who was usually an "unfree" tenant called a villein unable to leave the village without his Lord's consent, was given a holding of land consisting of both good and bad soils since the farming in open fields was a communal affair. This holding called a "carucate", plough land or "hide" – that is as much land as could be tilled every year by a great plough pulled by 8 oxen, averaging 120 acres – would be enough to make each family more or less self-sufficient, although the amount would vary according to the superiority of the household. Each year the "Court leet", composed of all the tenant farmers and the landlord would meet to decide which crops to plant in which furlongs, to regulate the grazing on the stubble after harvest, and which to leave fallow land. The common land also had to be regulated since this was not land common to all, as might be thought, but was owned by a landlord on which certain others had rights of grazing, etc. Even at this time the Anglo Saxons were already employing a method of crop rotation.

As an aside, it is interesting to note that at the time of the Norman Conquest through to 1349 when the Black Death decimated the whole country's population, Lincolnshire was second only to Norfolk as the most densely populated county in England.

As previously mentioned, at the time of the Norman Conquest, England was divided up into vills – each containing a group of houses surrounded by cornfields, grazing land, woods, meadows, etc. and each serving as a unit for purposes of law and taxation. To this Saxon organisation the Normans superimposed the system of manors which they had brought from Normandy. William the Conqueror had seized all the land of England into his own hands and distributed the greater part of it to nobles and warriors who came with him from France. They in turn gave estates to their friends and followers thus forming the manors. The manor house was surrounded by the enclosed fields of the "demesne", or home farm, which the Lord kept in his own hands and cultivated with the aid of his tenants and servants. The remaining land contained the open fields, commons and woodlands.

The earliest records state the land was given to Hago, the brother of William I, when he was made Lord of the Manor at Caistor. He it was who took the Caistor men to fight the Danes when they landed in Yorkshire about 1080.

Calling it Colesi, the village was mentioned in the Domesday Book and there appears to have been two settlements both with around 30 and 40 families inferring that the area was already well-established during the Saxon period. No mention of a church is made at this time. Evidence of possibly earlier occupation is provided by finds of three stone axe heads now housed in the British Museum. Another more gruesome find made in

1880 on land belonging to Westholme Farm on the north side of the canal were a great number of human skeletons and in an adjacent field many horse skeletons. One of the human skeletons had a spearhead transfixed in his skull.

In the early days most of present-day Lincolnshire came under the jurisdiction of the Danelaw and was divided up into shires. The area called Lindsey was sub-divided into three ridings which in turn were split into smaller divisions. Known as "hundreds" elsewhere, these were called wapentakes, the term coming from an Old Norse word, vapnatak, meaning a show of weapons at an assembly of freemen, to signify agreement to a proposal or resolution. Thus each wapentake would have been expected to provide a contingent of soldiers when required by the King. Until quite modern times South Kelsey came under the Walshcroft Wapentake.

Throughout the Middle Ages the village consisted of two fields and common land, together with some enclosed lands, called closes, which was typical of most villages of that period. The acreage of the parish was 4,198 acres, the vast majority of which lay in the two open-fields, carrs and commons. Only a little over 900 acres were already hedged and fenced about. The great bulk of these old closes stretched from the northern parish boundary south to the boundary with Thornton le Moor parish, within which closes lay the village itself. From the earliest days, each family would have had a small piece of enclosed land on which they would have built a hut, at first probably of mud and thatch, set alongside the road. On this land they would grow vegetables, keep a few hens, probably a pig, and even maybe a cow that would have been taken to graze on the common pasturage. This practice was known as "beastgate" or "cowgate" – that is, setting land aside to pasture a cow, or the right to pasture one cow on the common grazing before the enclosures. All this would have helped to feed the family while they laboured in the community fields.

A second large block of old enclosures stretched from the river Ancholme east along the southern boundary of the parish for about two and one-third miles. Three blocks of closes lay within the Carrs, the Warlott Closes and the Carr Closes. On the other side of the village at the eastern edge of East Field lay Nor Pale Close and Brick Close. Within the Furze Leas and Commons lay the Warren Closes and Ruffan Closes.

Going east across the length of the parish from the old river Ancholme, one crossed first the low-lying Carrs (about 495 acres), then having crossed through the village closes which separated the two open arable fields, one traversed East Field (c.690 acres) and then entered Furze Leas (c.285 acres) and the extensive Commons (c.1055 acres) on the poor light sandy soils. This last large area would now cover the land between the Market Rasen/Brigg road and the edge of Nettleton's Big Wood.

In the Public Records of 1276, Joan, widow of John de Hardrishille, petitioned the King and Council, that the keeping of her husband's lands be delivered to her as her husband held nothing from the King but only from the Chapter of Lincoln and the King's socage. An inquisition was viewed in Chancery as the King understood that he held the land from him "in chief by Knight's service", but in the Calendar of the Rolls 1272-1279, an order was given to the Sheriff of Lincoln to assign the land in North and South Kelsey to the petitioner as her dower.

At some point in the ensuing years, either by gift or by marriage, around the end of the 13th century the manor of South Kelsey came into the hands of Robert Hansard of Walworth Castle, Co. Durham who had fought valiantly for Edward I during the Scottish Wars. This would explain the stone effigy of a knight in 13th century armour and bearing the Hansard arms in the church of St. Mary's. A record also exists of Bishop Grosseteste granting a licence in 1236 for a chapel to be located on the Hansard family lands at South Kelsey. Because the Hansards appear to have been associated more with St. Mary's than St. Nicholas it is more likely that the licence was for the southern half of the settlement and could have been either for the building of St. Mary's or a small family chapel at the Hall. It could also suggest that the South Kelsey estates might at that time have been divided into the two parishes of St. Nicholas and St. Mary's, and would explain Joan de Hardrishille's claim to lands in South Kelsey in the latter half of the thirteenth century and other records indicating that the Monson family had holdings within the parish.

SOUTH KELSEY HALL

At some point, possibly some time in the mid fourteenth century, the Hansards built themselves a moated hall on the southern edge of the parish. In 1522 on the death of Sir William Hansard, the male Hansard line died out. However, Sir William Ayscough of Stallingborough acquired the wardship of Hansard's infant granddaughter and himself married the widow Elizabeth. In 1539 his own son and heir, Sir Francis Ayscough married the heiress, Elizabeth Hansard, when she came of age, thereby inheriting her estates. At that time, the moated site was altered and a new Tudor hall and gardens constructed within it. This served as the principal residence of the Ayscoughs, in parallel with that at Stallingborough, up until the beginning of the 18th century when Charles Ayscough died in 1706 without issue and the male line failed. It then passed by marriage to the Thornhagh family but it is unlikely that any of this family would have lived at South Kelsey in the 18th century since their family estates were in Nottinghamshire. At sometime during that century John Hewett /Thornhagh mortgaged the Kelsey estates and the Hall was later demolished and replaced around 1810 by the present farmhouse.

Of the Old Tudor Hall itself, very little remains apart from the moated outer court (though only the south arm is water-filled), part of one of the angle turrets (Grade II Listed Buildings) and some other fragments. The building was designed round a central courtyard and built of brick with stone dressings. The principal front, of which there is a drawing in the Gough collection at the Bodleian Library, was flanked by octagonal towers with domed roofs covered with lead. The site, together with its park, was described in detail in 1591, in a survey of the demesne of Sir Edward Ayscough.

At that time it is likely that almost the whole of the parish, encompassing the two open fields and common lands were the property of the Lord of the Manor. The only exception would be those belonging to Winghale Priory, although it is recorded that at some time the Ayscoughs were renting these lands.

WINGHALE PRIORY

The second block of closes previously described mainly comprised the site of Winghale Priory – sometimes called Wenghale, Wengall or even Wingle They were situated in the southwest corner of the parish running from the River Ancholme along the southern boundary. The site has yielded large quantities of Middle Saxon pottery together with Roman and Iron Age materials, turned up in shallow gravel quarries near the farmstead, confirming the antiquity of the site.

The origins of the monastic community are rather obscure, but presumably lie in an endowment made shortly after the Norman Conquest. The Domesday Book refers to it as King's land but now belonging to Roger of Poitou (aka Roger the Pictarien). He was the 3rd son of Roger de Montgomery, Earl of Montgomery and Shrewsbury, and was granted 298 manors by William the Conqueror. He was described by a contemporary as a prudent man of moderate temper, and a great lover of equity – a discreet and modest man. He died in 1094.

By 1103-4, William Count of Mortain had formally granted his manor of Winghale to the abbey of St. Martin of Marmoutier at Tours on condition a community of Benedictine monks should be established there. A priory was thus dedicated to St. John, as a cell to the Abbey of Sees in Normandy and the lands in South Kelsey, (one carucate and 4 bovates) , held on the annual service of one sparrowhawk. The priory was probably built around 1115 but it is doubtful whether it supported more than a handful of monks, one being the prior who acted as bailiff for the estate. Very few records survive of this Priory but names of its priors include Geoffrey de Ormano, John de Croquet and Michael de Logge. In 1400 the land appears to have been granted to a secular clerk.

The Priory was dissolved by Henry V and taken into the king's hands in the early fourteenth century. Finally in 1441 Henry VI gave the reversion to St. Nicholas College, Cambridge. It was then exchanged for tenements with Trinity College in 1443 and finally confirmed to them in 1461, but some land later passed by exchange to Sir Thomas Monson.

It is recorded that in the early 1400s, a daughter of Sir Richard Hansard of South Kelsey Hall married John Monson living at Winghale Priory and holding the Manor of South Kelsey St. Nicholas while in 1611 Sir Thomas Monson of Winghale was administering the South Kelsey estates probably during the minority of the 16-year-old heir, Edward Ayscough. Prior to that in around 1530, the wealthy Sir William Ayscough is known to have rented Winghale Priory for 40 years at £5 a year, along with several other local properties.

Around 1637, another reference to the Monsons is made when Sir John Monson brought in Dutch workers to drain the carrs along the Ancholme by constructing the New Cut from Bishopsbridge to Horkstow. He was probably living at Owersby at the time but Winghale was also mentioned and the work certainly would have affected the lands adjacent.

One family is recorded at Wingale in the diocesan survey of 1583 and buildings are shown on the site on maps of 1794 and 1847, approximately at the position of the present farmstead.

Throughout its history the actual ownership of the Winghale lands is difficult to establish. At the time of the Land Enclosures Act in 1794 Trinity College was still cited as the owner and a large block of old enclosures along the west side of the parish boundary, including the priory site, were identified as priory lands The lessee was one Mr. John Scott of Market Rasen who had a 20-year lease running from October 1788 which was allowed to stand. The only common land allocated to Trinity College under the Act was 65 acres of carr lands bordering the Ancholme.

In 1933, Trinity College, Cambridge, still owned College Farm (aka Nunnery Farm) next to the Priory lands at the side of the Waddingham Road, but it was formerly the property of the Benedictine nunnery of St. Leonards, Grimsby, which used to be sited at Nuns' Corner in Grimsby.

The original monastic buildings have long since disappeared and the site is now occupied by farm buildings. Earthworks indicating the site of the priory buildings are almost non-existent but three paddocks are defined by broad well-marked ditches and the remains of a fishpond complex can also be seen south of the farmstead. A rather gruesome find made when the farmer started to dig for gravel was a large number of human skeletons – presumably those of the Benedictine monks. It was the custom of the monks to bury their dead in the bare earth, but one was found amid stones and the remains of a shroud, perhaps that of one of the Priors. The first of these remains was noted as early as 1847 and continued to be found for nearly a century until the gravel pits fell into disuse. The bones were usually left where they were, but at one time the farm foreman had a collection of six skulls in his cellar until his wife objected!

Although the Winghale property lies within the parish boundaries, it appears that the land was not included in the South Kelsey Manor estate, but was variously owned by others throughout the centuries.

THE MEDIEVAL VILLAGE

A very large proportion of Lincolnshire's population through the Middle Ages were peasants, men and women who cultivated small areas of land chiefly for subsistence, and which they held as tenants or sub tenants of great lords or minor gentry. As such they were subject to both royal and ecclesiastical jurisdiction and to the manorial courts and the lord's power of punishment. They also owed him a series of duties ranging from small annual payments to the performance of labour services, sometimes as much as three days every week. It was also in everybody's interests that roads, bridges, banks and ditches were maintained and those who failed to carry out their responsibilities would have been fined at the manorial court.

From the earliest times, it had been the custom for all Christians to set aside a tenth part of their goods to the service of God. This translated into the tithes received by the rector each year to keep the church in repair, assist the poor and show hospitality to visitors. The priest was granted a house, a certain amount of land (called the glebe) and a yearly sum of money, chiefly derived from the tithes. The Church was the centre of medieval community life and saints' days would find the villagers gathering there in holiday mood after the special service to eat and drink around the building.

The central green, such a feature of many English communities, is missing from the majority of Lincolnshire villages, most of them (like South Kelsey) being built on a "rectangular" plan along the main street with additional dwellings tucked in behind as required. South Kelsey was what is called a "poly-focal" village – one cluster at the north end within the northern parish boundary formed by Deal Beck then beyond the dip, where another stream may well have run, to St. Nicholas church. Here a large number of dwellings was built along the side of the north/south road, and the last group of cottages stretched east/west from the crossroads at St. Mary's and southwards towards the Hall. The scattered nature of the community was further emphasised by the fact that for several centuries it was divided into two parishes – that of St. Nicholas and St. Mary's – until the Land Enclosures Act of 1796 when they were combined and the church of St. Nicholas demolished.

The houses and cottages in the village were each situated in an enclosed area of ground known either as a toft (back yard) or croft (back garden and paddock). It was here that hens, chickens, geese and ducks might run. There would be a space for vegetables such as peas, beans, leeks and onions as well as native herbs, important ingredients of a peasant's diet.

NOTE: In 1589 Elizabeth I passed a law proclaiming no rural cottage was to be built or building converted for habitation unless each was provided with at least 4 acres of land. These plots were actually smallholdings supporting livestock and growing corn, as well as vegetables. The Enclosure Acts drastically reduced the size of these plots as the landlord enclosed even more land.

No houses of that period survive, but they would have been small one or two roomed single-storey dwellings containing a hall and chamber and probably had a shed for implements and tools, pig, a cow and hens. Freemen would live in a 2/3 roomed house with farm buildings grouped around a crew yard where animals were over wintered and from which the manure was collected to spread on the fields. The latrine pit was situated conveniently, if not hygienically, close to the door, as would the well or waterpit, and the midden which would also have provided manure for the fields.

Local building styles reflect local materials and here where there are limited resources of building stone (only used for more important buildings such as the church and manor house) a tradition of building earth and timber houses developed over the centuries. Thus the villagers' houses would have been of 'mud and stud' construction. Although similar versions appear elsewhere in the country this is unique to Lincolnshire If available, a single layer of stones was first pounded into the earth and the studs, upright oak posts, were rested on 'padstones' thus preventing the earth from rotting the base of the wood. Next came a layer of handmade bricks on which rested the sole plate, another horizontal oak beam. A further beam was laid on top of the studs and a mid rail placed in between. All the vertical beams were then nailed together with laths of rough wood, probably riven ash. The "mud" was formed by trampling on a mixture of soil, clay, lime, water and straw placed in a pit. The straw bound the mixture together and the lime made it set. It was then daubed on to the laths both front and back to form a wall about 25 cm. thick resulting in a structure very similar to reinforced concrete. A coat of lime wash might be applied for further protection. Rafters would then be slung across the walls and a roof of simple construction built, usually half hipped and thatched with reeds or straw.

Inside the floor was beaten earth and the walls bare, with an open hearth for cooking and heating and an opening in the roof for smoke to escape – chimneys were a later innovation Furnishings were minimal – bed (straw and brushwood on the floor covered with a rug), table, a bench and stools. Dishes, mugs, plates and bowls would have been of wood or earthenware. What window openings there might have been were very small, unglazed and perhaps protected by wooden or possibly leather shutters. When weather permitted much of the cooking would have been done outdoors.

With sheep being such a feature of the Wolds landscape, wool would no doubt have been available for converting into cloth while villagers would grow their own hemp or flax, known as "line" or lyne. This would have been woven into a coarse cloth from which, until the introduction of cheap cotton, they would have made into clothes and other items for everyday use, while nettles were sometimes used in the manufacture of cloth. Every woman would have learnt how to spin, while men usually did the weaving. The hemp would also have been used in ropemaking.

From mediaeval times the universal garment for male agricultural workers was the smock.   Made from undyed linen or much later from heavy cotton twill known as "duck" these were the modern equivalent of overalls, covering their clothes and to some extent able to keep the wearer dry.   The basic design was cut out in rectangles to use every scrap of fabric, but the shaping was achieved by smocking which being slightly elastic made for ease of movement. Front and back were often made the same and could be reversed when one side became worn or dirty. The smock usually had a collar, cuffs and flapped pockets which were then covered in quite intricate embroidered patterns in self coloured thread. The making of smocks was a normal requirement of the country wife and the intricacy of the embroidery would be a matter of pride in her work.

During the winter evenings the men would sit around the fire carving wooden platters, bowls and spoons, weaving baskets from the local withies and fashioning articles from the tanned leather hides. They would repair their farm implements and make ropes and halters from the home-grown hemp.

Stews and pottage, an oat–based stew with added beans, peas, turnips and parsnips and sometimes leeks grown in their own garden, were their main food. Meat seldom appeared in the peasants' diet – the cattle were mostly kept for dairy products, milk, butter and cheese (although ewe's milk was often used for cheese). Salted beef was sometimes available as for centuries it was the custom to slaughter most of the cattle in the autumn and preserve the meat, due to the lack of cattle fodder during the winter months. It was not until the end of the sixteenth century that the idea of growing turnips as cattlefeed enabled more cattle to be over-wintered.

Although sheep were traditionally kept on the rough common lands and upon the Wolds, mutton was seldom eaten as the sheep were scrawny and tough and valued more for their fleece and for their milk to make cheese. Chickens would have been kept in the yard and pigs were also a valuable source of meat, as they were capable of finding their own food summer and winter and could be slaughtered throughout the year. These would have provided the fatty bacon which fuelled the peasants' labours in the fields.

It should be remembered, however, that all these products would have had to be shared with the Church and the Lord of the Manor who would have demanded tithes and rents in kind.

The hunting of deer, and boar before their extinction in the time of Henry VIII, were favourite pastimes of the landed gentry, together with hare coursing, but foxes were regarded as vermin and a record in 1590 exists of a person at South Kelsey being paid one shilling to exterminate them.

Deer, boar and hare, together with the rabbits which were farmed in the Lord's warrens, therefore belonged to the Manor, and severe penalties were imposed on any one found poaching them. However, the peasants were allowed to catch hedgehogs and squirrels. Fruit, nuts and berries were collected from the woods, preserved and stored.

Since there was obviously an abundance of fish (several fisheries are recorded along the banks of the River Ancholme) the family might occasionally have enjoyed such fish as perch, pike, roach and burbot. Eels and lampreys were also a great favourite in the middle ages. Again, the Lord reserved the exclusive right to any salmon or trout caught.

Another source of food came from the duck decoy. They are known to have existed in the marshes along the Ancholme although their exact location has not been established, but at one time there was a house called Decoy House just north of West Holme which suggests that there might have been one there. The decoy was a pond, roughly square, with tapering outlets at each corner which were fenced and netted to form traps and the wild ducks were then lured in and caught. Again, this and the ducks caught would have belonged to the Lord of the Manor.

The Lord of the Manor would almost certainly have had a dovecote in the Manor grounds where doves and pigeons would be raised for food.

Since ale was drunk in large quantities – in preference to the dubious water supply – there were brewers in every village. Small ale, that brewed for just two days, was drunk by all the family as the only safe thing to drink. Brewing was often carried out by widows and spinsters as a way of supplementing their income, selling the ale from their cottages as indicated by the display of a bundle of brushwood tied to pole outside the door – the first alehouses. Barley and oats were turned into malt and the Lord employed ale-tasters to check the finished product and to exact a licence fee from the brewers. In the fifteenth century, the Dutch, of whom there were many settled in the Eastern Counties, introduced beer. This was made from a malty liquor made bitter with hops which had the added advantage of preserving the liquor for longer - previously ale had always to be drunk within days of brewing. It took some time to become popular in England for many thought it had been poisoned, but eventually it began to supplant the traditional English ale.

The other main staple food was bread. Only the Lord of the Manor could have afforded to eat white bread made of wheat. The peasants would have eaten a dark, heavy bread made from rye and wheat, very often sown together and known in this part of the country as "maslyn". In hard times the flour might occasionally include beans, peas and even acorns.

During the medieval period, mills were governed by "milling soke", part of each manor's charter. The mill was the property of the Lord of the Manor, who as a result had a monopoly over the milling no matter who originally built the mill. It was however the Manor Lord's responsibility to have enough mills to meet the needs of his people and to handle major repairs. When the windmill was introduced the church became involved in the windmill business – Pope Celestine III claimed that the air used by windmills came from God and was therefore owned by the Church and consequently they must be built with the Church's consent and papal tithes paid for their operation. Whether this papal edict was observed here in South Kelsey is not recorded.

Tenants of the manor were obliged to grind their corn at the Lord's mill at a fixed rate of tool in kind – usually $1/16^{th}$ of the estate grown corn . The Lord's corn, of course, was ground free and given priority. A fine could be imposed on anyone caught using a quern for grinding cereals at home. Only if the mill fell into disrepair could tenants have their corn ground elsewhere.

There is only the sketchiest documentary evidence of corn mills in the village. There would almost certainly have been a watermill somewhere in the village, possibly on the old Kelsey Beck which ran through the valley from Moortown along the route of the later canal. The only known water mills appear in the nineteenth century – one on the disused Caistor Canal and the other at Watermill Farm on Nettleton Road Another is marked on the 1797 Enclosures Act survey map sited on the bend of Mill Road east of the village There must have been other earlier mills but no mention can be found. Initially it would have been owned by the Lord of the Manor but when this ceased to be the case, probably around the end of the 15th Century, it would have been owned or rented privately.

The windmill was not introduced into Britain until the late 16th early 17th century. There is the symbol of a post mill at the north-east corner of the old East Field and labelled Mill Close Mill marked on a map dated 1792 and on the Land Enclosures Map of 1797, but by 1828 this had disappeared and a new post mill had been built at the junction of North End Road and Brigg Road – another high point. Post mills were of wood construction and it was quite common for one to be dismantled and some or all of it used in the building of a new one. Because the position of the post mill could be moved so easily, may account for the lack of information on their location.

The miller was an important person, ranked third in power after the Lord and parish priest, as people were dependent upon him for their bread. Families sometimes worked a mill through several generations, the millwright's skills passing from father to son. They also had a reputation for dishonesty – the miller's "golden thumb" referring to the practice of pressing his thumb on the scales when weighing the corn to increase the amount and thus the toll paid.

The miller would almost certainly have combined the job of miller with that of baker. As the cost of building a bread oven was in most cases prohibitive for individuals, the village would have a bakery built and owned by the Lord with a "common oven" as it was called. Here the baker would either bake bread to sell or bake the peasant's own dough. As long as the baker did not demand unreasonable charges it remained a communal convenience. Again the Lord would have expected a share of any profits. Prices had to be posted or a miller could be fined 20 shillings. This was done to eliminate the illegal practice of "hanging the cat" whereby the miller took some of the farmer's corn for himself.

Each village also had its own smithy for making iron implements and housegear as well as small artefacts, and there would be at least one carpenter plying his trade. A rope maker was also a familiar sight in most communities using locally grown hemp.

Around the village were the communal arable fields and pastures. The low-lying marshes would have provided rich summer pastures for cattle, but would have been unsuitable for sheep as wetland encourages foot rot and liver fluke. However, the slightly higher ground towards Nettleton and the Wolds, although designated for rough pasture and rabbit warrens, could have supported flocks of sheep while pigs foraged in the woodlands. Sheep have been one of the chief products of the Wolds from the earliest times leading to the gradual development of their own breeds particularly suited to the terrain the most well-known being the Lincolnshire Long Wool.

Rabbit warrens were also an important part of the agricultural economy in North Lincolnshire. Warren farming gave a good return on poor soils with only a small capital outlay. A warrener was employed to manage the warrens and extra hands brought in at killing time, which lasted from the second week in November until Christmas when the skins were in prime condition.

The warrens were usually efficiently fenced with sod walls capped with bundles of furze. These did not last for many years, but the warrens themselves were most productive when frequently moved. Then the ground would be ploughed up for one crop of corn, followed by a crop of turnips followed by a sowing of "artificial grasses" such as clover, which would be grazed by sheep the first year and then turned back to rabbits. They were bred for their skins, especially the prized silver-skins (although they must also have provided a useful source of meat) which furnished the hat-trade and furriers in London. Another process involved scraping the fur off the pelts to make felt which was also used in the hat trade.

In this area, the skins would have been taken to Brigg where it was said there were more people engaged in dressing rabbit skins than in any other provincial town in the country. At this time foxes were seen as vermin and rewards were paid for killing them. There is a record in 1590 of one shilling being paid to someone to destroy foxes. There is documentary evidence of a sixteenth century warren existing in the Deer Park attached to South Kelsey Hall with the charming name of the Conny Gree (Conny presumably being a corruption of the old word for rabbit – "coney"). Mention was again made in 1771 when the park was described as having "the liberty and franchise of free warren" but was probably destroyed with the creation of landscaped parkland in the early 19th century.

The rabbit skin trade probably peaked in the 1780s when a silver grey fur could fetch as much as 1s.3d. but the fur trade was still in operation during the first part of the nineteenth century until the new Lord of the

Manor, Philip Skipworth, in return for an allotment of land, gave up his "right of warren" in 1811. It was then discovered that the land occupied by the warrens was particularly fertile and most were ploughed up as more productive systems of cultivation were introduced.

It is unlikely that water supplies would have been a problem to the villagers. The water table was high and springs running down from the Wolds fed the becks and rivers. Old maps show numerous wells in and around the village.

In early Tudor times all able-bodied men and boys had to practise archery regularly and a supply of arms was kept in every village, very often in the church. Later, training was also required in the use of the new firearms, but it was said that the Lincolnshire man showed little inclination or aptitude in the use of the clumsy hand guns and in their unskilled hands could prove as dangerous to friend as to foe.

The village would have been almost entirely self-sufficient – only salt for preserving food brought in from the salt pans at the coast, and iron for the smithy would have had to be imported from elsewhere. Pedlars would have travelled from village to village with small "luxury" goods, while the villagers would have gone to the nearest local market to exchange their surplus products.

It is difficult to assess the size of the village in the very early days, but the Parish Register dated 1563-6 (now sadly lost) contained a return by the Archdeacon of Lincoln quoting: St. Mary's Rectory – 57 families; Hamlet Wingale – 1 family, and Kelsey St. Nicholas Rectory – 31 families. It is interesting to note that Winghale hamlet is quoted separately – not listed under either St. Mary's or St. Nicholas's, even though it only consists of one family.

It does appear that the village escaped the worst ravages of the Black Death which regularly swept through England in the Middle Ages because it was always described as a large rural settlement and at no time showed any marked decrease in population. However it is unlikely they came off completely unscathed and when in 1590-1 and 1593 the plague carried off a number of the local residents of Caistor, Wragby and Cadney, South Kelsey must have suffered some losses of life.

THE LORDS OF THE MANOR

When William the Conqueror defeated the English army lead by King Harold in 1066, he had to take control of all of England before he could call himself King. It would have been impossible to rule the whole country personally and anyway, as Duke of Normandy, he had to return to France at regular intervals to retain his control there. After forcibly seizing all the land for himself and thereby dispossessing all the Anglo-Saxon aristocracy, he proceeded to divide the country into very large plots of land much like the counties of today, which he then "gave" to his French noblemen who had fought for him in battle and could therefore be considered loyal to him. In return they had to swear an oath of loyalty to William, collect taxes on his behalf from their area, and provide the King with soldiers if required. These barons, earls and dukes were known under the feudal system thus introduced as "tenants-in-chief".

But even they would have found governing such large tracts of land difficult and so the barons further divided up their land and "gave" it to trusted Norman knights who in turn had to swear allegiance to the baron, collect taxes and provide soldiers, at the same time keeping the resident English under their rule. These knights were called "sub-tenants" and the smaller plots of land were known as Manors. At all times the land continued to be held by the King and Baron or knight could be re-possessed by him.

Under the feudal system the peasants were totally answerable to the Lord of the Manor. He was the arbiter of local disputes, meted out justice and penalties and could command tithes and labour. No peasant was allowed to leave the village without his consent and every aspect of his life was governed by the rules of the Lord. It was not until the Black Death carried off nearly half the population of England that the surviving peasants were able to have some say in their own destinies and able to move a little more freely between villages. The early days of South Kelsey Manor are rather obscure and it is difficult to establish who the first Lords were but at some point in the thirteenth or fourteenth century it came into the hands of the ancient Hansard family of Walworth Castle, Co. Durham, and the Hansards and later, the Ayscoughs, were to hold the land for the next five

LORDS OF THE MANOR – 1400-1800

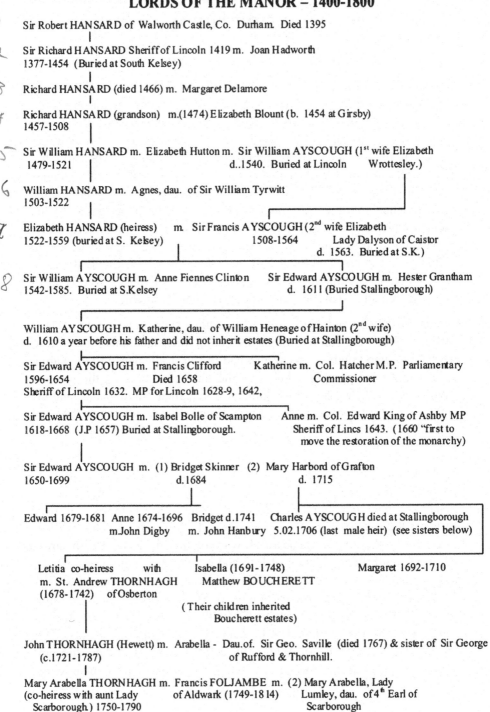

1 Sir Robert HANSARD of Walworth Castle, Co. Durham. Died 1395

2 Sir Richard HANSARD Sheriff of Lincoln 1419 m. Joan Hadworth
1377-1454 (Buried at South Kelsey)

3 Richard HANSARD (died 1466) m. Margaret Delamore

4 Richard HANSARD (grandson) m.(1474) Elizabeth Blount (b. 1454 at Girsby)
1457-1508

5 Sir William HANSARD m. Elizabeth Hutton m. Sir William AYSCOUGH (1st wife Elizabeth
1479-1521   d..1540. Buried at Lincoln   Wrottesley.)

6 William HANSARD m. Agnes, dau. of Sir William Tyrwitt
1503-1522

7 Elizabeth HANSARD (heiress)   m. Sir Francis AYSCOUGH (2nd wife Elizabeth
1522-1559 (buried at S. Kelsey)   1508-1564   Lady Dalyson of Caistor
                                                       d. 1563. Buried at S.K.)

8 Sir William AYSCOUGH m. Anne Fiennes Clinton   Sir Edward AYSCOUGH m. Hester Grantham
1542-1585. Buried at S.Kelsey   d. 1611 (Buried Stallingborough)

William AYSCOUGH m. Katherine, dau. of William Heneage of Hainton (2nd wife)
d. 1610 a year before his father and did not inherit estates (Buried at Stallingborough)

Sir Edward AYSCOUGH m. Francis Clifford   Katherine m. Col. Hatcher M.P. Parliamentary
1596-1654   Died 1658   Commissioner
Sheriff of Lincoln 1632. MP for Lincoln 1628-9, 1642,

Sir Edward AYSCOUGH m. Isabel Bolle of Scampton   Anne m. Col. Edward King of Ashby MP
1618-1668 (J.P 1657) Buried at Stallingborough.   Sheriff of Lincs 1643. (1660 "first to
                                                      move the restoration of the monarchy)

Sir Edward AYSCOUGH m. (1) Bridget Skinner (2) Mary Harbord of Grafton
1650-1699   d.1684   d. 1715

Edward 1679-1681 Anne 1674-1696 Bridget d.1741 Charles AYSCOUGH died at Stallingborough
                  m.John Digby   m. John Hanbury 5.02.1706 (last male heir) (see sisters below)

Letitia co-heiress   with   Isabella (1691-1748)   Margaret 1692-1710
m. St. Andrew THORNHAGH   Matthew BOUCHERETT
(1678-1742)   of Osberton
                              (Their children inherited
                               Boucherett estates)

John THORNHAGH (Hewett) m. Arabella - Dau.of. Sir Geo. Saville (died 1767) & sister of Sir George
(c.1721-1787)   of Rufford & Thornhill.

Mary Arabella THORNHAGH m. Francis FOLJAMBE m. (2) Mary Arabella, Lady
(co-heiress with aunt Lady   of Aldwark (1749-1814)   Lumley, dau. of 4th Earl of
Scarborough.) 1750-1790   Scarborough

centuries, passing it down through inheritance or marriage. Throughout his time, the Lords of the Manor were influential figures, holding high office in Lincolnshire, the surrounding counties and at Court. They owned extensive lands in other parts of the country and must have commanded vast wealth.

THE HANSARD FAMILY

The first records show that South Kelsey Manor had come into the hands of the ancient family of Hansard of Walworth Castle, Co. Durham, sometime in the early fourteenth century. Two old but undated memorials in St. Mary's church are attributed to this family - one of a lady and a knight in full armour (thought to be Sir Richard Hansard, Sheriff of Lincoln in 1419 and his wife Joan who lived at South Kelsey Hall) and the other a stone effigy of a knight in 13th century armour bearing a shield with the Hansard arms. This was possibly Robert Hansard of Durham who distinguished himself in the Scottish Wars during the reign of Edward I (1271-1307) and it is possible that it is at this time the King gifted the manor of South Kelsey to Sir Robert for his services during those wars. A record exists stating the South Kelsey estate was held by the Hansards "of the honour of Lancaster" which suggests it was gifted to them by the tenant-in-chief, the Duke of Lancaster.

The Hansards, known as the "Handsome Hansards" suffered mixed fortunes during the fourteenth century after the Black Death had swept through England and nearly half the population were wiped out. In 1367 the Manor of Walworth appeared in the hands of Ralph Neville, but in 1391, Robert Hansard, 9th in line to the title, reclaimed his estates for his 14-year-old son, Richard.

Sometime during this century South Kelsey Hall, a moated and fortified manor house was built on the southern boundary of the South Kelsey estate, and Sir Richard Hansard, 10th in line, and his wife Joan are known to have been living there in 1419 and proceeded to lay the foundations of the Hansards wealth. He died in 1454 and he and his wife are said to have been buried at South Kelsey. His son, 11th in line, died in 1466 whereupon his 9-year-old grandson succeeded to the title. When he too died in 1508, his son, Sir William Hansard, 14th in line to the title, was fighting under the banner of St. Cuthbert, when the English defeated the Scots on Flodden Field.

He was an extremely wealthy man, as his will revealed and it can be assumed that he madesome sort of financial contribution to the campaign and its victory.

In 1485 a mysterious but virulent disease suddenly appeared in England. It came on quickly the main symptom being excessive sweating and shortness of breath, earning it the name "sweating sickness" and within hours the sufferer had usually died. Few survived Five major epidemics occurred during the next century until the last known record in 1578. It then disappeared from England and to this day no-one has been able to establish exactly what it was or what caused it. In 1517 the third and possibly the worst epidemic broke out and in many towns in England nearly half the population was wiped out by the disease. Around 1520, in the wake of this epidemic, Sir William Hansard, then Sheriff of Lincoln, at just 42, died of the sweating sickness at South Kelsey leaving his widow, Elizabeth, as executrix of his will. Within a year his 19-year-old son and heir had also died of the same disease leaving his wife, Agnes, who he had married when he was 15, four months pregnant. In October 1521, she gave birth to a daughter Elizabeth, who was granted the estates of Walworth Castle and South Kelsey, as 16th in line. However, this was the end of the direct male line of the South Kelsey branch of the Hansard family although other branches of the Hansards, bearing the same coat of arms were still living in Lincolnshire up until the present day.

THE AYSCOUGHS OF STALLINGBOROUGH

For many decades it was possible to find members of the Ayscough family in prominent positions at Court. In 1438, William Ayscough was made Bishop of Salisbury. He was also Clerk to the Council to Henry VI and when the King came of age became one of his chief advisors, and the King's Confessor. On 23rd April 1445, it was the Bishop of Salisbury who performed the marriage ceremony of Henry VI to Margaret of Anjou. Such honours however sometimes bring danger and when the King's policies became extremely unpopular, three senior members of the King's inner circle were targeted. In 1450, during the Kentish Rebellion, Jack Cade's mob plundered and destroyed the Bishop's Palace at Edington in Wiltshire and William Ayscough was dragged from the church where he was celebrating High Mass and taken to the summit of the Downs and stoned to death.

The Ayscoughs were originally from Bedale but, when John Ayscough married Margaret Tailboys in 1463, they inherited the Stallingborough estates. Forty years later, in 1501, when his grandson, William Ayscough of Stallingborough (Sheriff of Lincolnshire 1499) was invited to attend the marriage of Prince Arthur to Katherine of Aragon, he was knighted by King Henry VII along with 56 others. Before his death in 1509, his heir another William was married to Elizabeth, the daughter of an influential courtier, William Wrottesley of Reading. Although the main seat of the Ayscough family was at Stallingborough, an estate a couple of miles inland from the Humber and just west of Grimsby, the couple set up home at Nutthall Manor in Nottinghamshire, which the Ayscoughs had inherited by marriage into the Cokefield family and held from 1469 to 1612. Young William spent much of his early years at the court of Prince Henry who was just four years or so younger than he was. When Henry VIII succeeded to the throne in April 1509, old Sir William had just died the previous month and the new heir was summoned to Court to help with the coronation. His family continued living at Nutthall, although Stallingborough remained the principal "seat".

Over the years his wife, Elizabeth, gave birth to six healthy children although William was still spending much of his time at court. In 1513, he went to France on campaign with the King and at Tourtaine was himself knighted by the King after the Battle of the Spurs. Seven years later in 1520 he travelled to France again to attend the lavish Field of the Cloth of Gold – a great honour.

On his return to England in 1521, as a well-favoured knight of the King, he was appointed Sheriff of Lincoln to become the King"s "ears and eyes in the county" succeeding to the post on the death in January of his old friend, Sir William Hansard of Walworth and South Kelsey. Sadly, the same year, his wife of fifteen years died after giving birth to their daughter, Jane.

Hansard left a widow, Elizabeth, his son and heir William, aged 19, and 15th in line to his estates, and two younger daughters, Elizabeth and Bridget. Young William had married Agnes, daughter of Sir William Tyrwitt of Kettleby, when he was only 15 but on 15th April 1521, he too died only a year after his father. However, his wife Agnes was already four months pregnant and in October gave birth to a daughter Elizabeth. Whilst her grandmother had been made executrix of Sir William"s will, the infant Elizabeth became 16th in line and heiress to all the Hansard lands at Walworth Castle and the manor of South Kelsey, and she was automatically made a Royal Ward of Court until she should come of age. This system of making wealthy minors Wards was a useful source of income for the King who assumed the custody of their lands and the authority to arrange his or her marriage.

In 1523, Sir William Ayscough, although still at Court, had kept in touch with events in Lincolnshire and petitioned the King for the wardship of the infant Elizabeth, at the same time proposing marriage to the widow Elizabeth. Although Sir William Tyrwitt, the child's grandfather and her closest male relative, also laid claim, Sir William proved the highest bidder making a lifelong enemy of his aggrieved neighbour.

Thus Sir William Ayscough gained control of the Hansard lands which were conveniently situated between the Ayscough estates in Lincolnshire and Nottinghamshire. South Kelsey had good lands and commanded a long stretch of the river Ancholme with all its fishing and fowling rights. It was centrally situated within easy reach of the market towns of Gainsborough, Market Rasen, Kirton-Lindsey and Caistor and to the main Lincoln/Barton-on-Humber road. Soon after his marriage he moved into South Kelsey Hall and managed to lease Wingal Priory for 40 years at 5s. per year and several other neighbouring properties. He also had the houses at Stallingborough and Nutthall, and owned Ayscoughfee Hall near Spalding (so called because the land on which it stood was held in "knight's fee" from the Crown) where he spent two months each winter at which time the larders were well-stocked with wildfowl. The Hall had originally been built by a wool merchant called Richard Alwyn in 1420 but granted to Sir William by Henry VIII. In fact, he owned lands in every corner of Lincolnshire, as well as Nottinghamshire and York and his wife's inheritance in Durham, becoming one of the wealthiest and most influential men in the County at that time. He also sat with John Heneage as MP in the Reformation Parliament of 1539.

In 1536 he became an unwilling participant in the ill-fated Lincolnshire Rising, or Pilgrimage of Grace, but quickly managed to disassociate himself from the protestors and after swearing an oath of allegiance was pardoned by the king. (See Story of the Pilgrimage of Grace).

He held very liberal views on the new Protestant religion spreading through the country and at Court, often coming into conflict with his more traditional Catholic neighbours when meting out justice in his various administrative roles. He ensured that his sons had a good education and found them places at Court, his son Edward was made Cupbearer to King Henry VIII, and arranged advantageous marriages for his daughters. Unusual in those days, he also encouraged his daughters to become well-educated and outspoken women which was to cause a great deal of trouble to the family in later years. (See the Story of Anne Ayscough) In the last two years of his life he suffered a debilitating illness, but continued to fight it until the end.

Before his death in 1540, he had already arranged that his own son and heir, Francis, should marry the heiress, Elizabeth Hansard, when she came of age, which he had done the year before, thus ensuring the Ayscough's claim to all the Hansard lands.

When Sir Francis came into his inheritance he pulled down the old moated and fortified house built by the Hansards and erected a modern Tudor house built mainly of brick. A record of a letter exists dated 1552 from Sir Francis to Sir William Cecil, the Principal Secretary of State to Edward VI, suggesting that the Church of St. Mary's at Grimsby should be pulled down and that Sir William should have the lead and he would "crave the stone and timber at a reasonable price". Whilst on a commission enquiring into "popish" activities in local churches he also acquired the altar stones of Market Rasen and Waddingham as building materials. The house itself was not completed until the beginning of Elizabeth I's reign.

Francis had been born in 1508 and was knighted by Henry VIII after the Battle of Boulogne. He was made Sheriff of Lincoln in 1545, 1549 and 1555 and continued to increase and consolidate his own lands. After the death of his wife Elizabeth Hansard in 1558 he made another advantageous marriage to Elizabeth Dighton, Lady Dalyson, the widow and heiress of the neighbouring landowner, whose land he had long coveted – that around Caistor. She died in May 1563 and he died not long after on 19th October 1564. A bust of him adorns his tombstone in Stallingborough Church.

Sir Francis had eight children by his first wife and two more by his second. After the death of his mother in 1558 and his father in 1564, his eldest son, William born in 1542 inherited, as 17th in line, all his father's vast land holdings and made a seemingly good marriage by marrying into the nobility. However, Anne, the daughter of Edward Fiennes Clinton, Earl of Lincoln, not only squandered the considerable Ayscough fortunes but failed to provide him with an heir. In 1579, he was obliged to sell Walworth Castle and its associated holdings to Thomas Jenison, who was Auditor General for Ireland at the time. When he died in 1585 his younger brother, Sir Edward, succeeded to the title. In 1587, the Ayscoughs sold their Manor of Holton-le-Moor to Othowell Bestoe of London, Merchant Taylor, which eventually came into the possession of the Dixon family in 1840.

When Sir Edward died in 1611, (he also was buried at Stallingborough) his eldest son and heir, William, had already died the year before and so it was his grandson, Edward at the age of 16 who succeeded to the

Ayscough estates. Like several of his family, Edward was well-educated and had gone to Cambridge University where he studied at Sidney Sussex College. It is said that Sir Thomas Monson, who resided at Wingale Priory at that time, was administering the South Kelsey estates for a short period in the early part of the seventeenth century, possibly until the young Edward Ayscough reached his majority.

When Charles I came to the throne in 1625, the 30-year War in Europe had already been gathering momentum for seven years and England had joined the hostilities the previous year. Faced with raising substantial funds for the war and a Parliament who refused to vote him sufficient taxation for military supplies the King sought to raise money independently. He invited his subjects to lend money but when this was a spectacular failure, he introduced the "forced" loan in autumn 1626 which, with no prospect of being repaid, was flagrantly illegal. As one of the leading landowners in the County, Sir Edward Ayscough, grandson of the former Sir Edward, was appointed a loan commissioner but joined with others in refusing to pay. However, on being threatened by a court of Privy Councillors that they risked "his Majesty's high displeasure" they reluctantly paid the full sum demanded.

In 1628, Sir Edward was elected to Parliament as member for Lincoln City, but the members proved so troublesome and unco-operative that Charles dismissed them and decided to rule without their help. By then England was no longer involved in the 30-years War and the King turned to local government for support.

In 1630, the rector of South Kelsey-St. Nicholas, Francis Rawlinson, died naming his old friend, Sir Edward, a beneficiary of his will with instructions to use the money in the founding of Caistor Grammar School and making him and his heirs patrons of the new school. (See the story of Caistor Grammar School)

In 1632 Sir Edward was Sheriff of Lincoln and played a major part in the administration of the County. By April 1640, after a turbulent eleven years of personal rule, Charles was forced to recall Parliament and Edward Ayscough was among 12 Lincolnshire members to be elected. The so-called Long Parliament commenced introducing many radical changes to the traditional role of monarchy and before long Parliament itself was dividing into two factions, Royalist and Parliamentarians. Sir Edward, considered by a contemporary as "one of the religious and sound men of the House", but with bad memories of the "forced" loans, sided with the Parliamentarians.

By early summer 1642, the two sides were gathering armed forces and Parliamentary troops were sent to arrest 17 leading Royalist gentlemen and disarm all other "malignants". In an effort to pre-empt this move, a band of Royalists, under the leadership of Sheriff Heron, was ordered to raid the house of parliamentary supporters and confiscate their arms. Thus, on 4th October 1642, they searched the home of Sir Edward Ayscough MP, at South Kelsey and carried off their booty to Cressy Hall at Surfleet. However, they were intercepted by a Parliamentary force and the Sheriff was arrested.

On 11th April 1643, the Royalists won a resounding victory at Ancaster Heath and to emphasise the point, proposed to indict for high treason the leading Parliamentarian supporters in Lincolnshire. These included Sir Edward, his brother-in-law Col. Thomas Thatcher, his son-in-law Col. Edward King of Ashby and his fellow MP Sir Christopher Wray. This turned out to be an empty threat and Sir Edward and Sir Christopher Wray, continued to administer the County, at the same time complaining bitterly to London of the negligible support they were receiving from Parliament and against "those gentlemen of great estate" who had abandoned Lincolnshire for the safety of Hull and London.

The conflict continued with first one side and then the other taking control of the county's resources and the countryside was often ravaged by lawless bands of soldiers from both sides but eventually it came mostly under Parliament's control. It is tempting to wonder whether the large number of skeletons of both humans and horses found in 1880 at West Holme farm on the outskirts of the village were the result of a Civil War skirmish.

When the war finally came to an end in 1649, the King was executed and England was declared a Commonwealth. Parliament was "purged" of dissenting members and the so-called "Rump" Parliament ruled until their dismissal by the Army in 1653. After the Army coup, of the ten MPs for Lincolnshire, only two took their seats; Sir Edward was one of four who were "secluded" and four more refused to attend the House.

During the Commonwealth era, a Government edict was issued ordering the destruction of all depictions of saints, the crucifixion and all other Papist objects such as statues, stained glass and pictures, and the total destruction of all fonts. From St. Mary's church registers it can be seen that throughout this period no infant baptisms were performed, only the births recorded, nor were marriages sanctified by a priest. Instead, the banns were read and the weddings formalised by a local justice of the peace, in this village usually Sir Edward Ayscough.

When Sir Edward died in 1654 his eldest son and one of nine children, yet another Edward, born and baptised in South Kelsey, succeeded to the title. At that time his sister Anne was married to Edward King MP, a Parliamentary Commissioner (the same who had been indicted for treason in 1643) and who was said to have been the first to move for the restoration of the monarchy. He had also been associated with the 'moderate' Col. Edward Rossiter who represented the County in 1659 and who had negotiated with the exiled Royalists to restore the monarchy. Thus in 1660 Edward was himself knighted at Whitehall by the newly crowned King Charles II. He died in 1668 and was buried at Stallingborough.

The third Sir Edward, born in 1650, was also elected to Parliament in the reign of James II as member for Grimsby in 1685. He was married twice, first to Bridget Skinner and secondly to Mary Harbord of Grafton. He died in 1699, leaving a son Charles and three daughters. His widow, Lady Mary Ayscough, founded the first school in South Kelsey in 1712.

The Ayscoughs appear to have divided their time between their estates in South Kelsey and Stallingborough although one branch of the family still held the Nutthall Manor until around 1615. Stallingborough was situated on a small rivulet only a mile or so from the Humber estuary where there was a ferry and a lighthouse to warn shipping of the mudflats. It would have been easy from there to travel by sea along the coast to London when Court duties demanded. Looking at a modern map it can be seen that there is a direct route between South Kelsey and Stallingborough and it is tempting to picture the Ayscoughs' coach trundling over the Wolds as the family made their way from one estate to the other. Their children were baptised either at South Kelsey or Stallingborough, depending upon where the family were residing at the time, and four members of the Ayscough family were recorded as marrying at St. Mary's between 1569 and 1624. The first William Ayscough was buried there in 1585.

When Sir Edward's son Charles died without issue in 1706 seven years after his father, he was the last male heir of the Ayscough family and it was left to his daughters to share the estates. Anne married John Digby of Mansfield Woodhouse and Isabella married Matthew Boucherett of North Willingham whose family inherited much of the Ayscough's estates, and incorporated the name into their own.

A third daughter, Letitia, married Andrew Thornhagh of Osberton and Fenton. and she inherited the lands at South Kelsey. Letitia's son, John, was born around 1721 and educated at Queen's College, Cambs. His godfather, Sir Thomas Hewett (1656-1726), gave his estates in Shireoaks,

Notts, to him for "the term of his natural life" and on his father, Andrew's death in 1742 he inherited Osberton and in 1756 under the will of his godfather, Sir Thomas Hewett, adopted his name and inherited Shireoaks. In 1742 he was appointed Chief Forester of the Walk of Roomwood and Osland, and the following year became deputy Lieutenant of Nottingham, a post previously held by his father. From 1747-74 he was MP for Nottinghamshire, Sheriff of Nottingham in 1745 and Sheriff of York in 1787, the same year as he died. In 1744 he had married Arabella, daughter of Sir George Savile and sister of Sir George of Rufford and Thornhill and on John's death, their daughter Mary Arabella became co-heiress with her aunt, Lady Scarborough, of vast estates in Yorkshire, Nottinghamshire, Ireland and South Kelsey. In 1774 Mary Arabella married Francis Foljambe of Aldwark and went to live on her husband's estate in Yorkshire.

It seems unlikely that any of the Thornhagh family ever lived at South Kelsey since their family estates were in Nottinghamshire and Yorkshire and by 1771 John Thornhagh / Hewitt had mortgaged South Kelsey Hall to Robert Gunny, described as "His Majesty's Minister Plenipotentiary and Envoy Extraordinary to the Court of Berlin". The death of John Hewitt in 1787 brought to an end the male line of the Thornhagh family.

The Hall was finally sold around 1780 for £15,000 and the property demolished. From the Indenture at that time, the land is referred to as 'sometime Monson's Manor', which may refer to the time when the Monson family acquired some of the land belonging to Trinity College (i.e. Wingale). On the Enclosures Act survey map, all the land surrounding Wingale and South Kelsey Hall is depicted as enclosed fields and was not therefore included in the land awards but could nevertheless have formed part of the South Kelsey estate. The Manor of South Kelsey itself was acquired by Philip Skipworth at the turn of the century from Francis Foljambe whose wife, Mary Arabella Thornhagh had inherited it from her father.

FRANCIS FERRAND FOLJAMBE

The Foljambe family can trace their ancestry back to the mid 13th century and in the fifteenth century by a series of advantageous marriages acquired more wealth and lands in three counties although the main family seat was at Aldwark, near Rotherham, Yorks.

Francis Foljambe (born 9th August 1669) was married to Mary Worsley of Hovingham. Despite having five sons and eight daughters, when he died in 1752 and was buried in the family vault at Ecclesfield, his only surviving heir was Thomas, his third son. When he too died six years later without issue, the direct male heir was his 10-year-old grandson, the only son of his sixth daughter Anne. In 1747 Anne had married Mr John Moore, member of a Hull merchant family, and her only son, Francis Ferrand Moore, was born on 17th January 1749 at the Foljambe's family home at Aldwark. In pursuance of his grandfather's and uncle's wills, he took the name and arms of Foljambe by Act of Parliament and succeeded to their estates in Yorkshire, Aldwark, Hadworth, Steeton and Westow.

In 1774 he married Mary Arabella Thornhagh, great granddaughter of Sir Edward Ayscough and co-heiress to estates in Osberton, Sturton, Nottinghamshire, the Savile estates in Brierly, West Yorks, and Ireland, together with the manor of South Kelsey. Before she died in 1790, she had borne him seven children, five sons and two daughters. After his wife's death, Francis Ferrand married again to another Mary Arabella, daughter of Sir Thomas Lumley the 3rd Earl of Scarborough and first cousin of his first wife. She outlived him by three years. Both wives were linked by marriage to the Saviles of Rufford Abbey in Nottinghamshire.

Shortly after his first marriage Sir Francis had taken up residence at Aldwark and commenced improving and consolidating his landholdings. In 1800 he sold Steeton and his lands in Derbyshire and shortly after that those at South Kelsey and in Ireland, after which he bought up more land at Scofton and Bilby to add to the Osberton Estates. He was MP for Yorkshire in 1784, High Sheriff of Yorkshire in 1787 and MP for Higham Ferrers in Northamptonshire from 1801-10. He eventually moved to Osberton in Nottinghamshire, the old family seat of the Thornhagh and Hewettt families, and died there on 13th November 1814.

He was a keen huntsman and in a letter to his wife writes about riding through South Kelsey with the Brocklesby Hunt, and was known to have ridden with several well-known Hunts around the country. He also took an interest in various commercial enterprises.

Although he instigated the Act of Enclosure and was the chief investor in the Caistor Navigation project, both of which were to alter the face of the village forever, it is almost certain he never lived in South Kelsey at any time, preferring to live on his estates in Yorkshire. In any case, the

Hall had been demolished by that time and there was no other suitable establishment on the estate. He did, however, exercise his right as Lord of the Manor to gift the living of St. Nicholas to his cousin Thomas Francis Twigge of Bakewell who was also vicar of Tickhill. His eldest son adopted the name of Savile and the family name continues to this day as Savile-Foljambe.

It is interesting to note that the window in the belfry tower of St. Mary's was installed by Francis Ferrand's great grandson, Cecil George Savile Foljambe, in memory of his wife and infant son who died at Scofton, Notts, more than seventy years after the family had sold their estates in South Kelsey.

THE SKIPWORTHS

The nineteenth century was beginning to dawn, bringing with it many changes in the social structure of Britain. After more than five centuries of passing from generation to generation of landed gentry by inheritance or marriage, the estate known as the Manor of South Kelsey came on to the open market. No longer was it necessary to have a title to own land, only enough money for its purchase and wealthy tenant farmers began to dream of becoming members of the landed gentry.

Philip Skipworth (sometimes referred to as Skipwith) of Aylesby, came from a wealthy farming family on the Wolds. He himself built up a prize flock of sheep by selective breeding of Lincolnshire Longwools with Leicesters, and in 1798 paying as much as 600 guineas for the hire of one ram for one season from a Nottinghamshire owner of New Leicesters. He had further augmented his income by enclosure surveying and road-building.

He was also very patriotic and the Napoleonic Wars which had loomed over Britain for some time, prompted him to take an active part in the formation of the Lincolnshire Legion of Volunteers enrolled to defend the County from the threatened invasion of Napoleon, giving a large subscription and promising the personal service of his sons.

At the beginning of the nineteenth century he joined with George Tennyson and others, in the speculative purchase of the Lordship of South Kelsey, an estate of some 4,500 acres. He acquired the sole interest in the land in 1808 and built Moortown House (Grade II Listed Building) on the Market Rasen Road in 1816 for his family's occupation at the north east corner of his lands.

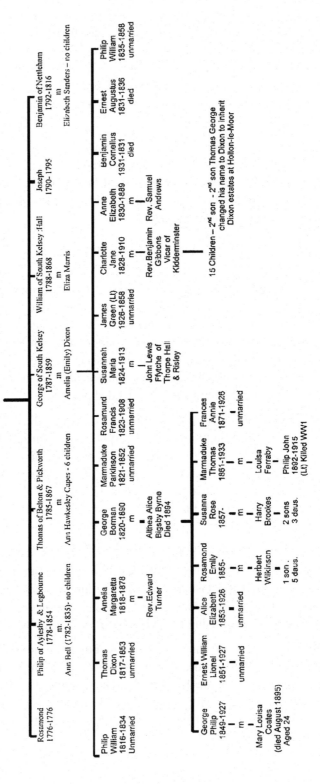

SKIPWORTH FAMILY TREE.

Philip SKIPWORTH m. Rosamond BORMAN (of Aylesby)
1745-1825   c 1752-1829

Philip's widowed brother, Thomas, who had farmed at Riby, moved to South Kelsey soon after its purchase and lived at Wingle Priory where he died in 1824.

When Philip died in 1825, his will gives a clear indication of how wealthy he was at the time. His eldest son Philip who had married Ann Bell and was already established on the lands at Aylesby and Legbourne had formally renounced any other inheritance in favour of his brother George. He was however bequeathed the sum of £4,000, with the curious proviso that he made no large provision for his wife. Can one detect previous hidden tensions between father and daughter-in-law? This same son had also inherited his father's flock of highly prized sheep, and in 1848 was known to have sold a flock of 400 ewes, the product of 80 years of selective breeding, for the princely sum of £1,500. He is also known to have been breeding improved strains of Lincoln shorthorn cattle.

His second son Thomas, had entered the Church by that time and must have been considered unsuitable to run a large estate. He had married Ann Capes and lived at Belton where an ill-advised scheme to process gypsum on his land ended in bankruptcy. Neglecting his parochial duties he was reprimanded by the archdeacon and finally was forced to retire to Pickworth.

To his fourth son, William, he bequeathed the sum of £5,000. William farmed 570 acres of the South Kelsey estate and lived with his wife, Eliza, at the newly built South Kelsey Hall (later called Hall Farm) while Philip's youngest son Benjamin married Elizabeth Sanders and lived at Nettleham.

To George, his third son, then went the bulk of his estates in Ashby, Burringham and Yaddlethorpe with further lands at Clixby, Grasby, Ashby-cum-Fenby, North Kelsey, Caistor and the manor of South Kelsey. He also arranged funds to pay all outstanding debts, although it is doubtful this was done as the estate continued to accrue debts throughout the century culminating in his grandson George Borman's bankruptcy. Provision was also made for his wife Rosamond to live in comfort for the rest of her life.

George had been sent to Wadham College Oxford and had already taken up residence at Moortown House in 1824, after marrying Amelia Dixon (Emily), daughter of the neighbouring Dixon family in 1815. He and his brother William, successfully farmed the estate for some years and hoped to establish themselves as members of the local gentry, but their more aristocratic neighbours tended to dismiss their social aspirations, despite their substantial landholdings and good education, because they were deemed yeoman farmers by working the land themselves, even in 1837 scathingly calling into question George's suitability to become a magistrate. He later proved his critics wrong by becoming the County's Deputy Lieutenant and also High Sheriff.

In 1852, with the coming of the railways, George sold several parcels of land in both North and South Kelsey to the Manchester, Sheffield and Lincolnshire Railway Company.

The 1851 Census reveals George Skipworth, aged 64, Deputy Lieutenant and Magistrate, living with his wife Emily at Moortown House with their five unmarried daughters, aged 20-26. They lived in some style still with a butler, footman, housekeeper, ladies' maid, two housemaids and a kitchen maid.

At the same time, brother William was farming at South Kelsey Hall and employing seven labourers and four indoor servants. He appears to have been a very respectable citizen, sitting on committees for the development of railways, as chairman of the Brigg Agricultural Society, and was even suggested as a Conservative candidate in 1852. When he died in March 1868 at 79 years old he was buried in St. Mary's graveyard. His widow Emily continued farming probably until she died in October 1875, when it was taken over by George Philip Skipworth. She is commemorated by a plaque in the church praising her as a kind and benevolent friend of the poor whose loss would be greatly regretted.

George died in 1859 and was buried in St. Mary's churchyard, his grave marked by an impressive tomb, which commemorates him, his wife and his children although all his married daughters were buried near their marital homes and at least two of his sons were buried elsewhere. Despite having a family of thirteen children, all his sons barring his third, George Borman, had predeceased him, including his two unmarried eldest sons and two who had died in infancy. Of his five daughters, four eventually married and moved away. His second daughter, Fanny, remained unmarried and stayed at home helping her father until his death when she moved with her mother to live at Risley Hall, Derby, the property of John Ffytche, of Thorpe Hall, who had married her sister Susannah Maria,

George's fourth daughter, Charlotte Jane, had married the vicar of Kidderminster, the Rev. Benjamin Gibbons, by whom she had 15 children. Their second son, Thomas George Gibbons, became the vicar of Wickham Bishop in Essex. He married Ethel Harriet (1862-1938) and they had 13 children. On the death of his cousin, Jamieson Dixon in 1906, he inherited the Dixon estates in Holton-le-Moor. He changed his name to Dixon but his children retained the family name of Gibbons.

When George Skipworth died in 1859, his only surviving son George Borman took over the running of the estate. In 1841 George Borman had been an attorney's clerk at Newark, but on 2nd May 1845 he was called to the bar, and became a practising barrister in London's Middle Temple. For nearly ten years he practised law, living in St. Pancras where he married Althea Alice Byrne and where three of his children were born but, on the death of his father and inheriting his estates, he and his family moved to Moortown House.

In 1872 he was known to have owned some 5542 acres in Lincolnshire and could have been deemed a wealthy man. However the following year he took up the cause of the Titchborne Claimant. This was a notorious fraud case which cost the country and private individuals many thousands of pounds. George Borman and others came forward to swear they had known the claimant in his youth and therefore could vouch for his right to the Titchborne inheritance. However, the judge did not believe George's evidence which so infuriated him that he made some very derogatory remarks about the judge and was in his turn convicted of contempt of court and fined £500. He refused to pay the fine preferring a prison term of three months during which time he attracted as much attention to his cause as possible. Initially he refused his friends' attempt to pay the fine for him, but eventually was released on payment of the fine. The local papers reported that he came home to the sound of church bells ringing and bands playing while triumphal arches were erected along his route. Whilst imprisoned he wrote a pamphlet entitled "George Borman Skipworth – on his imprisonment" a copy of which is held at the British Museum. At the same time, he had met four fellow inmates imprisoned for refusing to have their children vaccinated and after his release he was active in supporting those refusing compulsory vaccination.

However, legal expenses and his somewhat extravagant style of living set against a worsening agricultural depression caused him and his eldest son, George Philip, to borrow heavily against the estate.

When George Borman inherited the estate from his father, there was already an outstanding loan of £50,000 incurred by his grandfather, Philip. In 1870, he and his son borrowed a further £26,000 against his 4,875 acre estate and again in 1876 and 1879, £24,000 and £5,000 respectively. He would still have been receiving the rents from 87 properties in South Kelsey and a further 10 properties in Moortown and Caistor, together with the farm lands. There was also income from the Ancholme Commissioners and other properties and land in Thornton and Waddington. However, it would seem that he was unwilling or unable to pay back any of the money he had borrowed over the years.

Failing to meet the terms of repayment, he and his son were eventually taken to court in 1888 and ordered to pay a staggering £120,990.13.6d. to their creditors, specifically on Saturday, 8th December, between the hours of 12 and 1 at the Chapel of the Rolls in Chancery Lane, London. However, no-one turned up and George Borman and his son George Philip, were ordered to forfeit all their possessions and their estates were put in the hands of Trustees. George Borman died two years later at the age of 70. Although the estate was then in the hands of trustees, George Philip and his brother Lionel were still recorded as living at Moortown House as tenant farmers as late as 1904, before moving elsewhere when the South Kelsey Estates were bought by Walter Boynton.

George Philip and his brother Lionel were both born in London and went to school at Bury St. Edmunds. George Philip then went on to Cirencester Royal Agricultural College where he gained a Diploma and the Haygarth Gold Medal.

In 1881 he was farming at South Kelsey Hall, and in 1891, still unmarried, his household included his widowed mother, brother Lionel, sister Alice acting as housekeeper and his sister Frances as governess to three of sister Rosamond's children. In 1894 at the age of 44, he finally married Mary Louise Coates who sadly died just 11 months later at the age of 25.

A small tombstone close to the Skipworth tomb marks her grave. After living at Moortown House with his brother Lionel and sister Alice as tenant farmers until 1904 he is known to have been living at Tattershall in 1914 and was present at the opening of the village recreation ground in memory of his Aunt Fanny in 1922. She had left him a small legacy in her will when she died in 1908. He died in 1927 at a Sanatorium in Switzerland and it is thought possible that he made a second late marriage.

Another son, Marmaduke Thomas, born in 1865, was also educated first at Bury St. Edmunds and then at Clifton College a public school in Bristol. At 19 he returned to South Kelsey where he married Louisa Ferraby in 1887 and their son Philip John was baptised at St Mary's in 1892 while his parents were living at Moortown House.

In the Baptism Register, Marmaduke's unlikely occupation was described as "lemon grower". This probably refers to the fact that at some time he was known to have lived in Florida where he was presumably engaged in the citrus growing industry and where he must have made some money as he described himself as "retired" at the age of 39. His only son, Philip John Skipworth became a lieutenant in the First World War and was killed in 1915 at the age of 23.

Frances and her sister Alice became the proprietors of The Lodge Tearooms at Tattershall in 1919 and both died around 1926. Of the other two sisters, Rosamund Emily married Herbert Wilkinson who described himself as of "independent means" and originating from Kensington, London. They had one son and five daughters while Susannah Rose married Harry Brooks of Croxby and emigrated to Canada where they had five children, but the male Skipworth line died out with the deaths of George Philip and Lionel.

THE LAST LORD OF THE MANOR

Because George Borman Skipworth had been declared bankrupt his lands were conveyed by the trustees to the Equitable Life Assurance Co. in November 1894, but in 1904, the lands were mortgaged to Walter Boynton, a wealthy colliery agent, of Harbrough, Lincs, who paid £59,000 to Equitable Life and assumed the title of Lord of the Manor. Although the Boyntons may have lived in South Kelsey for a while, records show that by 1918 they were living at Lea Hall, near Gainsborough.

Mr. Boynton also owned lands in North Kelsey, Thornton and Waddingham, but in 1910 was declared bankrupt for failing to pay back a loan. The appointed trustees then conveyed the South Kelsey estate to his wife, Annie Boynton, who appears to have owned other land in her own right and in 1912, she borrowed £22,000 from the Royal Exchange Assurance Co. against her holdings. In December 1921, much of the land mortgaged to the Royal Exchange had been conveyed to L.W.G.Montefiore of London, but both Walter Boynton and his wife were still named as joint beneficial owners of the land known as South Kelsey Estates.

In 1922, the whole concept of Manor lands and the title of Lord of the Manor was officially abolished and the tenants were given the opportunity to purchase their properties and during the subsequent years many of them did.

In 1963, Montefiore's widow conveyed the land still known as South Kelsey estates, some 1,430.805 acres, to the Mercantile and General Reinsurance Co. Ltd. It included Kelsey House, Gravel Pit, School, Riverside, Sunshine and Caistor Road farms, together with various cottages and parcels of land. From 1971 to 1977 this company gradually sold off the individual properties to private owners and the once considerable estates of the Manor of South Kelsey finally disappeared.

THE LINCOLNSHIRE RISING & PILGRIMAGE OF GRACE 1536

After the Act of Supremacy was passed in 1534, a widespread Northern Rising against Henry VIII's religious policies was triggered in 1536 by the demolition of the smaller monasteries and the arrival of exchequer officials to assess and impose new taxes on the people. On 30th September 1536, fuelled by rumours that the King proposed to seize their Church jewels, the people of Louth gathered to protest and under the leadership of several men of standing rapidly gained supporters throughout North Lincolnshire. Joined by men from East Rasen and Horncastle they marched north and by 3rd October had reached Caistor where representatives of the various wapentakes had merely gathered to discuss the new subsidy with the commissioners, but were soon roused by a group of priests to join the Louth contingent.

Sir William Ayscough joined a party of the gentry, including Sir Robert Tyrwitt from Kettleby whose family still disputed Sir William's claim to the South Kelsey lands, outside Caistor on the road from South Kelsey. They seem to have been undecided as to their next course of action but made a hasty agreement to try and put the rising down. However, as they neared Caistor they were rounded up by the crowd and made to take an oath of allegiance. The rebels' leader, a gentleman called John Pormon, was quite specific about the commons' grievances. They were prepared to acknowledge Henry as Supreme Head of the Church, allow him first fruits and the new one-tenth tax on every benefice and even the subsidy already granted but "he shall have no more money of the commons during his life nor shall he suppress any more abbeys". They also demanded the death of the so-called heretic bishops.

Sir William Ayscough and his party were taken back to Louth where they composed a letter to the King outlining the commons' grievances and expressing their own fears for their lives and goods if the people were not pacified. Above all, they reiterated their own loyalty and asked the King's pardon for the rising when he had heard their grievances. They thus hoped to contain the uprising until a reply was received.

The King's brother-in-law, the Duke of Suffolk, had been sent by the King to diffuse the situation and stayed at some point at his wife's house at Grimsthorpe where Sir William and a group of gentry joined him "rejoicing that they had escaped the rebels".

Meanwhile the rebels had first marched to Lincoln and then northwards into Yorkshire and beyond where they gained even more support and under the leadership of Robert Aske, a lawyer, it became known as the Pilgrimage of Grace. This posed the biggest challenge to Henry's position, but he temporised by offering pardons to the gentry, thus splitting them away from the commons, and in the Spring of 1537, the King took his bloody revenge on the Pilgrims and many of the ringleaders were executed.

Sir William Ayscough and his gentry neighbours were eventually able to disassociate themselves from the uprising and having sworn an oath of loyalty to the Crown were given the King's pardon. The so-called "Lincolnshire Rising" had lasted no more than ten days.

ANNE AYSCOUGH – THE ENGLISH PROTESTANT MARTYR

Perhaps one of the most famous and well-known of the Ayscoughs, certainly around the time she was alive and sometime after her death, was Anne Ayscough, or Askew as she was sometimes known. She was the daughter of Sir William Ayscough and his first wife Elizabeth Wrottesley and was born at Nutthall Manor in Nottinghamshire, but on her father's second marriage to the widow, Elizabeth Hansard, she and the family moved to South Kelsey. Martha, Anne, Jane and their step-sister Elizabeth Hansard, grew up in the enlightened household of their father, Sir William and his second wife, the widowed Elizabeth Hansard. By the standards of the age they were very well-educated women and became fluent readers and writers of English and probably Latin. They would have absorbed all the new and radical ideas brought home from university and Court by their brothers and with Protestant influences strong in the household they were encouraged to form their own opinions.

By the time Anne was 12 years old, William Tyndale had translated the New Testament and most of the Old Testament into English and Sir William bought a copy. In 1539 the Great Bible was printed in English and a copy placed in every church, but in 1543 the Act for the Advancement of True Religion was passed which forbade all men below the rank of Yeoman and all women to read the Bible in public or in private.

Of all Sir William's children, Anne became the most committed to the new religious thinking. She studied Tyndale's New Testament which made a deep and lasting impression on her and even as a teenager was reading the Bible to the servants and villagers. In the meantime, her father was arranging advantageous marriages for his children. Francis and his stepsister were duly married around 1540 and Edward married Margaret, the young widow of George Skipworth, who had inherited considerable lands around Keelby and Nun Cotham, while Jane married George St. Paul of Snarford. The latter was a close friend of the Suffolks and was steward for their extensive estates in Lincolnshire. Jane lived happily at Snarford raising a large family and, after George's death, married Richard Disney of Norton Disney. When he too died, she returned to South Kelsey where she lived until her death on 27th December 1590 and where she was buried.

Sir William's eldest daughter, Martha, was to marry Thomas Kyme, a wealthy fenland farmer, whose family owned extensive lands at Wrangle, Friskney, and Stockford and was closely related to Guy Kyme who had been executed for his part in the Lincolnshire Rising. Unfortunately Martha died before the marriage could be celebrated and, rather than forfeit the dowry and lengthy negotiations, Thomas asked to marry Anne instead. Thus in 1540 Anne, the outspoken Protestant zealot, was married to Thomas Kyme, a stubborn unimaginative Catholic – it could not have been a worse match.

Anne reluctantly moved into her husband's fenland home but found no-one to whom she could relate. Despite her husband's protests she publicly read aloud from the Bible to anyone who would listen and was dubbed "the fair gospellor", a new word which had just entered the English language. Despite bearing two children by her husband, she always referred to herself as Anne Ayscough, never accepting her married name of Kyme. By the end of 1543, the atmosphere was so impossible Anne decided to go back to the protection of her brother, Sir Francis at South Kelsey, no doubt to the relief of her husband. However, the ensuing scandal in his village persuaded Thomas to ask for her return but Anne refused, instead suing for divorce. She was turned down at Lincoln and in 1544 decided to take her case to the Court of Chancery in London.

At Court, Henry VIII was slowly dying. His sixth wife, Catherine Parr and her ladies, including Catherine Brandon, the Duchess of Suffolk, and Lady Elizabeth Tyrwitt of Lincolnshire, were all Protestant sympathisers while the household of Prince Edward was staunchly of the new religion. Lady Elizabeth was married to Sir Robert Tyrwitt, younger brother of Sir William whose daughter Agnes had married William Hansard. She had been governess to Princess Elizabeth, was a zealous Protestant and a close friend of Queen Catherine for the rest of her of life.

With her family connections, Anne easily entered the exclusive Court circles where she earned great respect for her enormous knowledge of the new Bible, while waiting for her divorce to be heard at the courts. The petition was eventually dismissed. She did, however, gain a formidable enemy – that of the Lord Chancellor of England who was trying to discredit the Queen and her followers. He compiled a damning dossier on Anne and on several occasions she was brought before the courts to answer charges of heresy and finally she signed a recantation in 1545.

Thinking that this would be the end of the affair and worn out by her ordeal she again returned to South Kelsey and her brother's protection.

In the meantime, her husband Thomas, criticised and goaded by local priests angered at Anne's release, decided to denounce her as a heretic. They were both summoned to London, but Thomas, knowing Sir Francis had influence at Court, asked the Bishop's office in Lincoln to fetch Anne from South Kelsey. When the Bishop's men arrived, Anne hid in a nearby cottage but unfortunately a note between her and her brother was intercepted and they realised that he must know her whereabouts. After questioning Sir Francis and his wife for several hours and under threat, Sir Francis reluctantly revealed her hiding place, an act of betrayal he appears to have regretted for the rest of his life. Forewarned of her danger, she hid her copy of the bible and fled into Kelsey Woods where she was finally captured and taken with Thomas to London. Here on June 19, the Kymes appeared before the Council at Greenwich where Thomas was dismissed but Anne was faced with fresh charges of heresy. Thomas finally washed his hands of her and returned home.

For the next eight days Anne was interrogated by the Council and, steadfast in her faith, categorically denied the legality of the Sacraments, thus condemning herself to be burnt to death   Her death sentence should have been the end of her ordeal, but on 29th June 1546 she was taken to the Tower where her interrogators wanted her to incriminate other members of her sect, in particular the Queen and her ladies. In a desperate attempt to get results she was subjected to the rack, a form of torture reserved strictly for male criminals and totally illegal for a gentlewoman. Despite repeated protests from the Tower's lieutenant her tormentors, Wriothesley and Rich, continued, but without success, until she was finally released. Her joints and muscles were so weakened she could not walk, but nothing would break her resolve. She was first taken to a private house in order to keep her illegal ordeal quiet but she was finally moved to Newgate where many more so-called heretics were housed.

During the weeks that followed she was able to write letters to her friends, together with long and detailed accounts of her two trials and interrogations, which were smuggled out of Newgate prison by her maid. Weakened by torture, Anne was carried to the scaffold on a chair and chained to the stake to keep her upright, but no doubt heartened by the band of supporters who openly accompanied her. Bags of gunpowder were placed around her neck and those of the three others who were to die with her which mercifully hastened their end amongst the flames. She was 24.

In the reign of Mary 1, after the death of her husband, the Duchess of Suffolk and her family were forced to flee into exile on the Continent.

Her accounts of her imprisonment and interrogations, *The First Examination (1546)* and *The Latter Examination (1547),* were both first published by Bale, who illustrated the work with his own *Elucidations* in which he praises her as a great English Protestant martyr and condemns her Catholic accusers. He paints her as an obedient, pious and virtuous woman (the popular male view of women in those days) but her writings reveal she was a strong, independent woman with a vast knowledge of the law and a deep conviction in her own beliefs, which with her courage and intelligence enabled her to expose the theological errors evident in the charges laid against her and to confound her male interrogators.

Ironically, three years later when Edward VI came to the throne much of what the new Protestants had believed and dared to say aloud were included in the new English Book of Common Prayer.

Throughout the centuries Anne has captured the popular imagination as one of the first great English Protestant martyrs and her story has been re-told many times.

A prayer Anne wrote a short time before her death, illustrates her courage and the strength of her faith:-

"O Lord, I have more enemies now than there be hairs on my head, yet Lord, let them never overcome with vain words, but fight thou, Lord in my stead, for on thee I cast my care. With all the spite they can imagine they fall on me, which am thy poor creature. Yet, sweet Lord, let me pay no heed to them which are against me, for in thee is my whole delight. And, Lord, I heartily desire of thee that thou wilt of thy most merciful goodness forgive them that violence which they do and have done to me. Open also thou their blind hearts, that they may hereafter do that thing in thy sight which is only acceptable before thee, and so set forth thy verity, without all vain fantasy of sinful men. So be it, O Lord, so be it."

Above Figs. 1-5: Thatched Cottages from before the War. Below Left Fig. 6: The Balderson Family outside their shop on the Crossroads and Below Right Fig. 7: Balderson's Bus - The First South Kelsey Bus

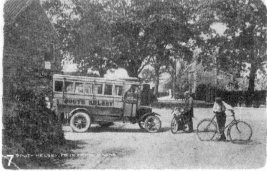

Left Fig. 8: The Kirby's Shop on Brigg Road **Above Right & Below** Figs. 9-11: The old Forge on Brigg Road the 1900s, 1920s and 1930s (with the Bicycle Shop on the left of the Bottom Picture).

Above Figs. 12-14: The Village Post Office, Thornton Road. **Below** Fig. 15: Moortown House 1938

Top Left Fig. 16: Caistor Road. The Methodi
Sunday School and School Farm.
Top Right Fig. 17: Caistor Road. Sunshine
Farmhouse showing the Butcher's Shop on th
end wall.
Above Fig. 18: The Crossroads early 1900s
"The Bull Inn" - note thatched roof. The cotta
on the right belonged to the Bacon family
before it was pulled down.
Left Fig. 19: Caistor Road - Looking towards
"The Bull Inn"
Below Fig.20: Pupils lining the railings of the
Village School.

Fig. 21: Manor Farm c. 1900
with ladies from the Green family.

Above Left Fig. 22: Hall Farm
viewed across the Moat.

Above Right Fig. 23: A nineteenth
century funeral bier.

Right Fig. 24: The Mortuary Chapel
in the graveyard of St. Nicholas
Church – it was demolished in
the 1980s.

25

26

Above, Right and Below Figs. 25-27 Old pre-War photos of the Old Rectory also known as the Old Vicarage. The building was destroyed during the Second World War.

27

Above Fig. 28: A Post-war photograph of St. Mary's Church showing the original pinnacles on the tower, taken down in 1987 for safety reasons. **Below** Fig. 29: The Thirteenth Century tomb of Sir Robert Hansard

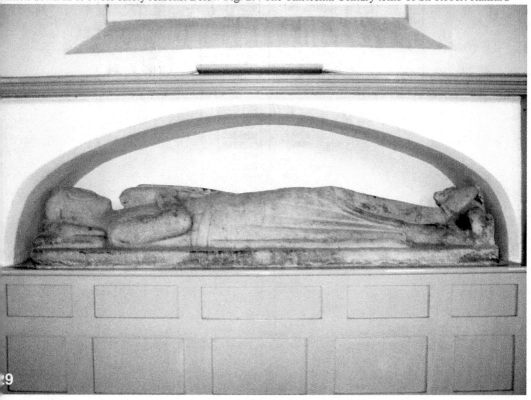

FRANCIS RAWLINSON AND CAISTOR GRAMMAR SCHOOL

Francis Rawlinson's name will always be known in this area as the founder of Caistor Grammar School, but his connections with South Kelsey are just as strong.

He was born in May 1564, the second son of Christopher and Joan Rawlinson, a well-established family of Market Rasen (or East Rasen as it was known then). He was baptised at the church there and was educated at the local school which was then situated between the present railway bridge and Oxford Street. He was a promising scholar and was sent to Clare College, Cambridge. Here he matriculated in 1580 at the age of 17, became a BA in 1583 and an MA in 1587. After he was ordained he became a deacon at Lincoln and then moved to Middle Rasen Drax in 1589 where he remained until 1603. This church has since disappeared.

He was to have been made rector of Waddingham St. Peter, but an unfortunate misunderstanding arose and the offer was withdrawn. He was nearly 40 years old and unmarried before he became rector of South Kelsey St. Nicholas, but within six months of his installation on 13th July 1603, he married the recently widowed Mrs. Helen Smith and became stepfather to her family of six children ranging in age from 18 to 3.

His living at South Kelsey, which would have been given to him by the patron of St. Nicholas, Sir Edward Ayscough, brought him in around £40 per annum, but through various family bequests, Francis inherited two houses and a not inconsiderable fortune which he carefully invested and preserved. For nearly fifteen years, Francis lived happily at the rectory with his wife and step-family, watching them grow, marry and leave home until his wife Helen died, leaving him with two unmarried stepdaughters still at home. However, one of them, Susan, was planning to marry Edward Eastland who had recently inherited his father's house at Branston. In a very convenient arrangement, Susan married Edward and moved to Branston, while Francis married the widowed mother, Faith, at Broxholme and she moved back with him to the Rectory. Once again he took on another ready made family of three more children.

The Rectory of St. Nicholas itself was situated close to the church and must have been a good size to have accommodated the Rector's ever expanding family. There was land attached to the house and more land in the common fields. The yards contained stabling, a large tithe barn and two buildings described as belfries. The Rector employed several men to work on the glebe land, as well as house servants. He also spent his own money in keeping the church of St. Nicholas in good repair. Records show that in 1610 the seats in the church were repaired and a communion table and chest were purchased, at a cost of £16, a considerable sum in those days.

When he died on 29th December 1630, he had just signed his will giving directions for the endowment of a school at Caistor. The instructions were very explicit – he gave £400 to Sir Edward Ayscough for acquiring land on which to build and maintain a free Grammar School for the people of Caistor on the understanding that the inhabitants themselves should build a Schoolhouse at their cost and to the satisfaction of Sir Edward Ayscough within two years of his decease. Sir Edward and his heirs were nominated as patrons of the school for ever and charged with electing a fit schoolmaster as often as was necessary, paying his stipend of £30 per annum from the income derived from the acquired lands.

If the inhabitants were to refuse to build the schoolhouse then the £400 would be given to Sidney Sussex College in Cambridge for the maintenance of four poor scholars.

However, the schoolhouse was indeed built within the two years specified although the exact details of who actually paid for it are unclear. It is possible it came out of the £250 bequest made by Hansard, as it is unlikely that the building itself cost more than £50. The original school hall built of ironstone is still in regular use by the present school. It is also more than probable that the land on which the building itself was situated, which was quite small, (15 poles) would have been donated by Sir Edward who was at that time also Lord of the Manor of Caistor and owned all the land thereabouts. It is known that the bulk of the £400 bequest was used to purchase land in Bilsby to provide revenue for the upkeep of the school and the schoolmaster's stipend.

At the same time, William Hansard of Biscathorpe (not South Kelsey although he used the same coat of arms), was a rich man and had had plans to found schools at both Caistor and Wragby, but was forestalled by Francis Rawlinson who died a year before he did. After much dispute, it was agreed that provision under Hansard's will should pay £15 per annum for the school usher. This would be financed by the purchase of a farm and lands at Cumberworth at a cost of £250.

Francis's will was a long and complicated document and contained innumerable gifts and bequests. All his stepchildren, their offspring, and his god children were remembered and Sir Edward Ayscough's five eldest children were left £5 in gold. He also left instructions for every poor household in his parish to receive one shilling in money, two pecks of barley, and their dinners at his burial plus 2d to be paid to each parishioner attending his funeral. Forty shillings was left for the repair of St. Nicholas church and twenty shillings each to Kelsey St. Mary and North Kelsey, along with several bequests to East Rasen. To his wife he left the use of a small cottage in the village for three years together with the sum of £60 to be paid within one week of his death. and some land in North Kelsey. The cottage had previously been bequeathed to his nephew, son of his brother Christopher, which would be given to him on reaching the age of 21 in 3 years time.

He died on 29th December 1630 and next day was buried, where he had requested, in the chancel of St. Nicholas at the east end of the communion table under the blue marble stone there.

THE FAIR YOUTH

A question that has puzzled scholars over the centuries has been the identity of "The Fair Youth" and "King" or "Prince" mentioned in several of Shakespeare's sonnets. A favourite candidate has always been a young man called William Hatcliffe

The Hatcliffe family were an ancient family of wealthy landowners with estates in Hatcliffe, West Ravensdale and Gunnersby. In 1567, Thomas Hatcliffe, heir to the Hatcliffe estates, married Judith, daughter of Sir Francis Ayscough, while his brother, George, married her sister, Elizabeth. The next year William Hatcliffe was born at South Kelsey Hall and baptised at St. Mary's church on 6th September 1568. He was said to have been gifted with exceptional beauty, intelligence and charm and in due course became a fellow of Jesus College Cambridge. As heir to an ancient line of gentry, and with good family connections, he was admitted to Gray's Inn, without actually obtaining a degree, at the age of 16. At the Christmas revels at the Inns of Court, he was elected Prince of Purpoole, or Lord of the Revels, where it was said he first met Shakespeare when presenting one of Gray's Inn's comedies in January 1587/8. This could explain Shakespeare's references to the Fair Prince in his sonnets.

As a young man he lived an extravagant life style and was soon in debt. When he married, his wife Dorothy Kay had little fortune of her own and in an effort to settle his debts his father made over the manors of West Ravensdale, Hatcliffe and Gunnersby to him Unfortunately he had no aptitude for running the estates successfully and continued to sink deeper and deeper in debt.

In 1609 he was said to have taken an unpublished manuscript of Shakespeare's Sonnets to London for publishing, but requested that the dedication should be discreetly disguised, thus perpetuating the mystery of the "Fair Youth's" identity. His fortunes never recovered and when he died around 1629 all his estates had been sold and the Hatcliffe inheritance lost forever.

THE ENCLOSURE ACT 1794

The most dramatic change in the history of the village was brought about by the Enclosure Act. Throughout Britain the enclosing of land had been going on gradually for centuries, with or without the peasant tenants' consent, but during the seventeenth and eighteenth centuries the Agricultural Revolution was in full swing and such enclosures were hastened by private Acts of Parliament initiated by the landlords who saw that the land could be used more profitably if it were enclosed in smaller fields. In 1794 the following Local Enclosure Act was passed:

"An Act for Dividing, Allotting, and Inclosing the Open and Common Fields, Carr Lands, Furze Leas, Waste Grounds, and other Lands in the Parish of Saint Mary South Kelsey and Saint Nicholas South Kelsey, within the Manor or Lordship of South Kelsey... and for extinguishing all rights of Common and Sheep Walks in and over the same". A notice of the intended enclosure of this parish had appeared in the Stamford Mercury in September 1793. The Act itself ran to 33 pages.

Three Enclosure Commissioners were appointed, all living in Lincolnshire, each receiving a daily fee of two pounds and two shillings (or two guineas as it would have been called then) for their expertise. A surveyor, Joseph Colbeck of Baulby in Yorkshire, was also appointed. By the standards of the day, the commissioners earned a great deal of money since, over the years, they could take on upwards of thirty commissions. As they usually had fair sized landholdings themselves with all the commitments that involved, the overload of work often caused considerable delays in settling claims when they took on too much work at a time. Moreover, not only did they command generous fees, they were also able to claim expenses incurred when travelling around the country. Many of these men left considerable fortunes attributable entirely to their Commission work.

The enclosure of South Kelsey then followed the general pattern of other similar Acts. The first step was to post a notice of the commissioners' meeting on the door of St. Mary's church, at which all persons must stake their claim, in writing, to ownership of land or right of common. Then the commissioners were to take charge of all farming operations ("direct the course of husbandry") during the process of enclosure and were empowered to impose penalties for any breach of their orders. The appointed surveyor would plan and build both private and public new roads within two years, for a salary paid for by the commissioners, and inform the Justices of the Peace when they were finished. All farm leases ceased and the commissioners fixed compensation to the farmers. The only exception was the lessee of Trinity College lands, some 60 acres. He was to pay £7 per centum per annum in addition to his rent until the end of his 20 year lease.

The rectors of the two ecclesiastical parishes within South Kelsey, the Rev. T. F.Twigge (St. Nicholas) and the Rev. Wm. Bowra (St. Mary's) were to be awarded glebe land and a corn rent in lieu of future tithes from all lands in the parish. This was to be equal in value to one-seventh of the open fields, one-ninth of the carrs, ings and warlotts, one-tenth of the commons and furze leas, and one-ninth of the old enclosures liable to tithes. A large area on the southern border surrounding South Kelsey Hall and Wingle Priory, together with three blocks of fields on the Carrs adjoining the river, and the village plots, were already designated as enclosed land and would not have been included but almost all of the remainder of the common land, some 2,925 acres, was awarded to the then lord of the manor, Francis Ferrand Foljambe. No allotment was made to the Free School, nor in respect of the Bull Meadow, or the Common Meadow, which are mentioned in some old books as belonging to the parishioners.

Up until this date the unit of one acre was not a fixed area and could vary considerably from district to district. At the time of the enclosures this was standardised throughout the country to the measurement recognised today.

With the abolition of the open field system, parcels of land were allotted to individual tenant farmers. These same farmers would often ask for land away from the village in order to build themselves a house on their own land. This explains the presence of isolated farmsteads at the end of their own private roads scattered around the parish, all dating from the early 1800s.

The loss of common grazing land would have a profound effect on the farm labourers. Most households would have had a cow to provide dairy products and, as the Lincolnshire breed was a large draught animal, could also be used to plough their strip of land. Now there was no common grazing nor land to plough, the cow would have to go, and another valuable source of income for the family, with the sale of dairy products, would be lost.

At around this time, an agricultural revolution was taking place - crop rotation was being introduced into the newly formed enclosed fields and better designed ploughs and farm equipment were becoming available, making the land far more productive. New breeds of sheep and cattle were being developed a notable one being that made by Thomas Turnell (1737-1811) of Reasby near Wragby, who crossed his large Lincolnshires with cherry-red Durham and York Shorthorns which became the now famous Lincoln Reds known all over the world.

It was also the time when the teams of oxen, that had always been used to pull the ploughs, were being replaced by horses which were employed until they too were replaced by mechanised tractors in the twentieth century. In 1892 it was recorded that the chief crops in this parish at that time were wheat, barley, oats, beans and turnips.

ROADS

The other major change to the landscape under the Land Enclosure Act was the building of roads. At that time, eight public roads were mentioned. Radiating out from St. Mary's Church was the Spittle (Waddingham), North Kelsey, Caistor and Thornton Roads. Mill Road running out to the Market Rasen Road was most likely North End Lane which no longer makes this connection for vehicles. The survey map clearly shows the Mill halfway along its length. Ancholme Road possibly ran along the side of the beck towards the river Ancolme. The Smithfield Bridle road, which ran from just north of the Moortown crossroads north east across the fields, was probably used by the villagers to take their animals to North Kelsey Moor, a 4,000 acre area of rough pasturage shared by the seven parishes adjoining it. The surveyors also mentioned a 50 ft wide public carriage road running north to south and crossing the Caistor Road at Moortown and known, as it is today, as the Market Rasen Road.

Not mentioned is the road sometimes called Sorrylease Lane and at others the Coaching Road, which ran from the Caistor Road across the fields to South Kelsey Hall, now just a track through the trees on the first left hand bend of the road out of the village. It is quite possible that this could have been the route the Ayscoughs would have used to travel to Caistor and then across the Wolds to their Stallingborough estate, a route still clearly traceable on modern maps.

Probably few people ventured eastwards towards the River Ancholme across the swampy ground to the frequently flooding river, but when the carrs were drained in the seventeenth century and the New Ancholme cut, a crossing, called Wingle Ferry, appears to have been provided to cross the river. When the Land Enclosure roads were put in, the east/west road would almost certainly have connected with the turnpike opened in 1765, which followed the route of the old Roman road from Lincoln via Caenby Corner and Brigg to Barton-on-Humber and thence by ferry to Hull. Branches from this road also went to Melton Ross and Caistor. A bridge is marked on the Enclosures Map of 1794 but this may have been replaced by the Toll Bar Bridge (still visible at the side of the modern road crossing the old river and recently restored).

The Surveyor mapped out and installed the road we now know running from Nettleton to Waddingham while the coaching road became a lane which is no longer in use. Eastwards the new road crossed the Market Rasen Road towards Nettleton and to the west down to the Catchwater Drain and crossing the old River Ancholme at Wingle Bridge (or Toll Bar). This latter half of the road was called Spitall (or Spittle) Road at the time. However from the old maps it appears the first road was planned to run almost straight from the church down to the Catchwater Drain to the site of the present Holme Hill Farm, (built around 1860) and then along the bank until it reached College Farm. Here it turned at right angles and continued down to Wingle Bridge crossing the Ancholme. The present road that turns left at the entrance to Holme Hill Farm and rejoins the old road at College Farm was obviously put in at a later date or the original route was never implemented. The bridge over the Catchwater Drain was sometimes known as Poverty Bridge

The road through the village used to run straight from the crossroads right up to North End, but probably at the time of the Enclosures Act was diverted to run on the loop road through the houses while the original road became a public footpath. There was also a lane running right around the Church at one time. Over the years modifications were also made to the road known as Park Lane adjacent to South Kelsey Hall, straightening it out and changing the entrance from the south side to the north. It was around this time that the Hall itself was falling into disrepair and would finally be demolished and replaced by Hall Farm in the first decade of the 19th century. Clay Lane, a track opposite to the new entrance to Hall Farm leads across the fields to Wingale Priory.

In 1860 mention is made of Sand Lane, running from North End to Moortown House Farm, being made good at the expense of the parish, while the occupants were to keep it in good order by paying for gravel from the gravel pit. This would have come from the gravel pit situated at Gravel Pit Farm, accessed by a track from the Brigg Road and which was probably in existence at the time of the Enclosures Act.

Roads, ditches and hedges had all to be constructed to strict standards laid down by the Commissioners and for a while created a lot of new employment for ditchers, hedgers and suppliers of quickthorn hedging.

These changes did not, however, occur overnight and as late as 1816, the new landowner was still in dispute with the authorities due to delays in completing the necessary work.

Like all roads built under the Enclosure Acts, it ran straight across the open fields only turning sharply at the end of the new boundaries. It was made approximately 40 feet wide to allow for deviations around muddy patches during the winter and edged with a ditch and quick growing hawthorn hedges interspersed at intervals with ash trees. In addition, it had to be fenced pending the growth of the hedge, the cost of which had to be borne by the landowners and could be quite considerable. The road itself remained the property of the Highways Commissioners who would rent out the wide verges for grazing or hay. This method of grazing sheep and cows was called "tenting" and the school logbooks during the nineteenth century record children being off school to look after the animals. In 1863 a resolution was taken (South Kelsey Vestry Minutes 6th January) that the money raised from the letting of the lanes "shall be paid to the Overseers of the Poor for the time being to be applied for purposes not allowed by the Auditor" after it was discovered that the accounts of the overseer were seriously in debt.

In the Vestry Minutes of 1865-66, it was noted that G.B.Skipworth was bringing gravel up the Caistor Canal to supply parishioners wanting gravel for private roads in the parish at a cost of 2d. a ton. There is also a mention of a gravel pit owned by Mr. Skipworth, possibly that at Gravel Pit Farm. It is also known that gravel was being dug at Wingle Farm around 1847.

When the roads were finally surfaced many years later, only the minimum was paved and the wide verges retained. These can still be enjoyed today as they provide a rich tapestry of wild flowers. Similar roads can be recognised all over England but in particular the Midlands, East Anglia and Lincolnshire.

WATERWAYS

The River Trent (the name meaning The Trespasser because of its habit of invading the surrounding land) had always throughout historic times been a highway for trade and communication. To the east, running parallel with it, the river Ancholme acts as the eastern boundary to the parish and the name probably derived from the British word for marsh and the name of the river Colne. It was another river that regularly flooded to a width of half a mile across the adjoining low lying land but now the Ferriby Sluice holds back the sea and much of the surrounding marshy land has been drained.

At the beginning of the seventeenth century, a traveller wrote describing the River Aukham (Ancholme) as a muddy little river and therefore full of eels, emptying itself into the River Humber. At one time it was also known to support colonies of beavers. The only crossings of the river were at West Rasen and at Glamford Bridge, (now called Brigg) the first mention of the latter being in 1203. As early as the thirteenth century land owners paid subscriptions for work to be undertaken with the aim of facilitating navigation and land drainage and the River Ancholme's charter is one of the oldest in the country but it was not until the carrs were drained in the seventeenth century that it became feasible to cross the old River Ancholme near South Kelsey, first by Wingle Ferry and then by a bridge already in existence when the Land Enclosure survey was carried out. Toll Bar Bridge, as it sometimes was called, was finally bypassed by the present road and is no longer in use although still visible at the side of the road. It has however recently been repaired at the instigation of English Heritage.

About the time the land round the Isle of Axholme was being drained, Sir John Monson, who also owned Winghale Priory, brought in Dutch workers to drain the carr lands along the river Ancholme and by 1637 the New Cut from Bishopsbridge to a sluice at Horkstow had been constructed. The canalising of the river certainly opened up a route from the central vale to the Humber and helped the expansion of Brigg but it was not entirely successful as a navigation until continued work on the river culminated in an Act passed in May 1767 created the New River Ancholme transforming a meandering water course to the dead straight canal it is today. A warehouse was built at Brandy Wharf in 1825, together with a pub, "The Anchor" (now the Cider Centre) and a number of cottages for bargees and warehouse staff. In 1835 a Weslyan Chapel was also built.

After John Rennie had carried out work on the Ferriby Sluice, further improvements took place in the 1820s, when several hundred men were at work along the whole length. Their lawless depredations were such that local inhabitants (and Kelsey must have been greatly affected, the river running as it does along its western boundary) complained that scarcely a duck or fowl of any size was to be found for some miles on either side of the Ancholme. Nevertheless, the work did make the river navigable for vessels of sixty tons as far as Bishop Bridge in the parish of Glentham. This resulted in an increase of trade and population in the villages along the valley (South Kelsey's population increased from 449 to 632 during the first 30 years of the nineteenth century) and provided an avenue of transport for the crops now growing on the recently drained lands. The horse boat from Bishop Bridge and Kelsey brought the country folks into Brigg market every Thursday and in the second half of the nineteenth century it was possible to take a passenger packet from Brigg to South Ferriby which connected with a steamer to Hull. Even well into the twentieth century, South Kelsey farmers were transporting their produce down to Brandy Wharf to load onto boats for countrywide distribution.

The original River Ancholme, now relegated to little more than a drainage ditch, still meanders through the carrs, and forms the eastern boundary of South Kelsey parish until it joins the new Ancholme at its junction with the Caistor Navigation. From there it continues its wandering course to the Humber via the town of Brigg, crossing and re-crossing the New Ancholme at several places. The New Ancholme no longer sees the passage of goods along its length but instead is a very popular waterway for pleasure craft. Holiday caravans occupy the west bank opposite the busy Cider Centre at Brandy Wharf.

The Deal or Dale Beck which makes its way unobtrusively into the north side of the canal just past the road bridge, forms part of the parish's northern boundary and bisects the land belonging to Dale Farm which, although geographically appearing to be in South Kelsey is in fact in North Kelsey. The mill pond for the water mill on Nettleton Road was fed by an offshoot of the Nettleton Beck originating on the Wolds. The mill stream continued westwards, crossing under the railway line until it turned south to join the Beck again just short of Moortown. Meanwhile Nettleton Beck, having passed under the road ran alongside it until it reached Moortown where it re-crossed the road and circled the hamlet before entering the South Kelsey Drain which followed the course of the old canal. Evidence of this explains the additional set of railings at the edge of the road beside the canal in South Kelsey.

THE CAISTOR NAVIGATION

Although now little more than a wide ditch, the Caistor Canal was first envisaged in 1792 when the economic advantages stemming from the post-1767 improvements of the Ancholme Navigation were realised. A Mr. Hall called the first meeting to discuss the project which was held on 3rd July 1792 at The George in Caistor. Concern was expressed about the adverse effects of drainage on the Ancholme Navigation and surrounding lands but these were resolved when it was agreed that all the local springs should be discharged into the head of the Canal to maintain an adequate water supply. William Jessop was asked to carry out a survey and a local solicitor, John Turner, was appointed as Clerk. A parliamentary petition was submitted by Lord Middleton and others on 18 February 1793 and on 3 June of the same year an Act was passed for "Making and Maintaining a Navigable Canal from the River Ancholme in the parish of South Kelsey... into the Parish of Caistor". It was to be used for the conveyance of coals, corn, wool and other goods, wares and merchandise to the advantage of Caistor and surrounding districts

To finance this project the proprietors were authorised to raise £15,000 in £100 shares, but very few shares were in fact sold. However, Francis Ferrand Foljambe, of Aldwark, (who at that time still owned the South Kelsey estates) in addition to purchasing shares in the company also agreed to loan the company £4,600 at 5% p.a. The project went ahead but it was noted by 1813 the tolls on the canal were insufficient to pay interest and arrears were rapidly building up. As late as 1828 shares were coming up for sale but no interest had ever been paid on them.

Construction work on the canal started in 1795 and took five years to complete, carried out under the direction of its engineer, Robert Dickenson. It left the New Ancholme four miles south of Brigg and ran for approximately four miles in an easterly direction, but never reached Caistor as planned. A lane laid out in anticipation of the completion of the canal leads from Caistor town centre to the proposed site of the terminal basin and is to this day known as Navigation Lane. In fact, the canal ended in a basin some four miles west of Caistor at Moortown on the Market Rasen / Brigg Road. The canal to Moortown was opened to traffic about 1800 and in 1801 an abortive proposal was made to extend it in a more southerly direction to Market Rasen.

There were six locks, with a total fall of 42 feet, from Moortown known as Moor, Mill, Willow, Ings and Beck End. The sixth unnamed lock lay near the Moortown basin. Between Mill and Willow Locks lay South Kelsey basin and bridge. The canal terminated at Moortown with a basin 100 yards long and 13 yards wide. The canal itself, together with its locks, showed a high standard of engineering and was built wide enough to accommodate the Humber Keel boats. Although it never fulfilled its original aims, the canal did for a short time provide an important link with the New River Ancholme, and the wharf at its termination in Moortown once annually distributed 45,000 tons of coal from the Midlands by the several coal merchants living in the area at that time.

In 1824, James Green Dixon of Caistor and Rothwell added a corn merchant's business to his farming. He stored corn purchased from North Wolds farmers in warehouses at Brigg and Brandy Wharf which was then shipped to Wakefield and Leeds and in return imported coal and animal feedstuffs for distribution locally. The house that stands at the Moortown crossroads was originally built as warehouses to serve the canal basin.

An open wharf was also built at South Kelsey on the east side of the road where it crosses the canal but no buildings appear to have been constructed beside it. While the canal was in operation a swing bridge was constructed where the Brigg road crossed the canal to provide passage for the barges sailing up to Moortown.

The canal bridge was replaced in 1964 by a new road bridge resting on the old foundations which it is said included some of the stonework from the demolished St. Nicholas church.

By 1819 a small brickworks had been built on the north side of the canal, no doubt taking advantage of the easy transport of bricks to the outside world, but also providing the hard red bricks used to build the majority of the nineteenth century houses in the village. This has now disappeared but its site is marked by a modern house built beside what was the old brickyard.

The land on which this property stands was cut off from the village by the formation of the canal, but is still within the parish boundary.

A small water mill was built at Mill Lock utilising the fall of water there after the canal had been closed in 1855. A photo of the mill exists, but no trace of the building itself remains. It did, however, grind corn and feedstuffs right into the 20th century.

With the advent of the railways in 1848, goods traffic diverted to this faster and more convenient method of transportation and in 1855 after only 50 years the canal finally closed to traffic. It did however serve a useful purpose as a means of land drainage until the early 1900s.

Nowadays, the canal is just a ditch and only traces of the locks remain. Moortown and South Kelsey basins were filled in and most of the canal now runs through private land.

In 1930, the Ancholme Drainage Board wished to take over the canal and made extensive searches to find any heirs to shareholders or company solicitors but without success.

The Company was finally wound up by a Parliamentary Order in 1936.

RAILWAYS AND ROAD TRANSPORT

The railway arrived in the area in November 1848 as a branch of the Manchester, Sheffield and Lincolnshire Railway Company, which later in 1923 (as the Great Central Railway) became part of the London & North Eastern Railway. It ran from Barton on Humber to Market Rasen to link with the ever growing network of railways across the country, The nearest station was at Moortown where the present railway crosses the Nettleton Road and the familiar railway house was constructed at the level crossing.

Moortown Station also served Caistor and at the beginning of the 20th century Mr."Bussy" Borman ran a regular horse-drawn bus service from Caistor to meet each train for which he charged 6d. return, 2d. for a child.

A reminder of the part played by the Skipworth family in the area is recalled by the Skipworth Arms public house built by the level crossing. Trains no longer stop at this point and the nearest station is at Market Rasen.

Despite the advent of the railway, South Kelsey inhabitants continued to use the roads as their chief method of transport and carriers with their horse drawn wagons continued to provide a service to the end of the century. The 1892 Kelly's lists Henry Martin, Wallis Barr and J. Hunt running once-weekly services to Caistor, Brigg, and Market Rasen on market days.

In 1919, Joseph Balderson bought his two sons, Henry and Edward, just returned from the War in France, a new Ford Model T bus from which modest beginnings they developed a bus and lorry service trading as Balderson Bros. until 1934. The vehicles were mainly Ford or Chevrolet (later to be replaced with Bedfords) and painted in a livery of red and cream. One multi-purpose vehicle conveyed pigs and sheep in a high sided open top lorry to market and on its return was quickly swept out and converted into a bus to convey passengers. They carried farm produce and requisites, coal and road making materials to and from local railheads, tarmac from Scunthorpe and passengers to local destinations. A regular passenger service was run from South Kelsey to Lincoln on Fridays, Market Rasen on Tuesdays and Saturdays, and Brigg on Thursdays and Saturdays.

After the partnership broke up, Eddie continued to operate a bus service until he retired in 1941 when both buses were sold to a Scunthorpe bus company, while Harry ran a bus and lorry service licensed to carry any goods, anywhere, for anyone.

The War years brought plenty of business to Harry – agricultural produce continued to be moved, along with sand and gravel for airfield construction and the somewhat unusual task of daily transporting German and Italian POWs from Willingham Hall to work on various farms in the district.

After the War, Harry's son, Cliff, joined the firm and the Company expanded. Haulage contracts included airfield maintenance, runway extensions, various missile sites, power stations, motorways and by-passes, Immingham docks, Cadwall Park racetrack extension and the Humber Bridge construction in the 70s. In 1972, Harry died leaving the business to Cliff who gave up the haulage business in favour of the motor trade garage business which now continues to be run by his son, Nick, on the site of the old haulage premises on Thornton Road.

Sometime during the 1970s, P.H Alltoft started up a family road haulage business on the Brigg Road in the village which is still in operation today.

At one time, a firm in Scunthorpe ran a daily service to and from Scunthorpe passing through Caistor and Grimsby. Services today are scarce with occasional buses to Lincoln and a supermarket bus to Brigg three times a week. Nowadays people in rural areas have to rely more and more on private transport for convenient travel.

POSTAL SERVICE

Sometime between 1856 and 1892 saw the arrival of a post office in the village and Kelly's directory around that date states that letters arrived from Caistor at 9.45 a.m. and were despatched at 2.55p.m. The nearest telegraph office was at Caistor. By 1933 letters were being routed through Lincoln. It should be noted that a Victorian post box is still in use set in the wall of what used to be the Old Bakery in Brigg Road.

A retired postman living in the village can still remember when he went on his motor scooter to the Moortown station to pick up the mailbags which were thrown out of the passing mail train that slowed down at that point. Then, balancing the mailbags precariously on his handlebars, he took the letters back to the post office (which also served as a general store) and was situated in the cottage on the bend of the road opposite the present Village Hall. Here he and the postmistress sorted the letters in a small shed behind the shop before delivering them by bicycle, or on foot in very bad weather, as far as Brandy Wharf and North Kelsey Carrs. Later he collected the mail from the post office in North Kelsey where it had been delivered by van but, with the gradual demise of rural post offices, a part-time post office opened at Windy Forge on Waddingham Road, finally closing in 1999. The nearest sub post office was then at North Kelsey but in 2007, this too was threatened with closure invoking an angry response from all the surrounding villages, but to no avail. In 2008 it was closed to be replaced by a less than satisfactory so-called "Outreach" service. Yet again, central government was to strike a blow at rural community life.

CRIME AND PUNISHMENT

In the early days, crime would have been dealt with by the Lord's court or by the Church, and in 1405 it was made obligatory to provide stocks for punishing a wide variety of offences - breaking the Sabbath, excessive drinking, blasphemy, or selling faulty goods could all result in the offender spending a few hours "stocked" to the mockery and abuse of the villagers. No record of South Kelsey's stocks exists, but they could well have been located near one of the Churches.

A curious Lincolnshire tradition finally died out during the nineteenth century. Known as ran-tanning, if a man was accused of ill-treating his family, the villagers would gather together and drag an effigy of the culprit around the village banging on kettles, pots and saucepans, anything that made a loud noise. Finally they would bring the effigy back to the culprit's house and burn it. In later centuries the Penal Code imposed savage penalties for what would now be considered minor offences, and imprisonment, hanging and transportation were common punishments. The Game Laws in particular, which limited the right to shoot or take game, including hares and rabbits, to landowners, were made even more rigorous and as late as 1816 a labourer caught with a net in his possession at night could be transported for seven years whether or not he was actually found poaching. Records in the 19th century show at least four South Kelsey men transported to Australia although the crimes are not mentioned. Sentenced at the Lincoln Assizes they were:-

1817 –   James Parker, aged 28, 14 years

1818 –   John Robinson, Robert Husker deported for life.

1841 –   George Elson, aged 26, 7 years.

MINING IN THE NETTLETON AREA

A coal mining operation was started around 1838 at Nettleton Moor but was unsuccessful while ironstone was discovered in 1860 at Holton-le-Moor, but not exploited by the land owners. Ironstone mining did, however, start at Claxby-by-Normanby in 1868 near Acre House Farm.

Since there had been no history of mining in Lincolnshire, experienced miners were recruited from as far away as Cornwall and Scotland. Local workers, including some from South Kelsey, were also employed but mostly in a less skilled capacity. A row of miners' cottages was built on the road to Claxby and a branch railway line constructed from the station at Holton-le-Moor to the bottom of the hill below the mine entrance Here it was connected to a small gauge track from the mine itself bringing out horse drawn tubs of iron-ore. The men were paid on the amount of ore they mined and often safety was ignored in the interests of earning more money. Many men were killed or injured and a local clergyman described it as that "gloomy cave of disaster" where scarcely a month went by without a fatality. Little was done by the employers in the way of compensation, but in order to help the families affected by death or injury and keep them out of the workhouse, many miners joined a Friendly Society at Caistor called the Snowdrop Lodge of the Free Gardeners. (See Friendly Societies chapter) When mining started up at Lincoln the Claxby mine was closed in 1885 after less than twenty years.

In 1928, with the growth of Scunthorpe Steelwork, mining started up again on Nettleton Top. It took nearly six years to carve out the hillside, lay new tracks to the mine entrance and construct a 6000 yards long aerial rope way down to the railway siding. In 1934 it was officially opened and continued until after the War when it had become a vast fully mechanised undertaking. Three huge tunnels were cut into the hillside containing 12 miles of railtrack and in 1960 alone, 200,000 tonnes of ironstone were being transported to the Scunthorpe Steelworks. In the late 1950s a second mine was opened at Nettleton Bottom in the next valley and a tunnel was constructed through the hillside to connect it to the original mine. For a while the mines were a major employer in this area, but in 1968 with the advent of cheap high quality iron ore from abroad, the British Steel Corporation decided to close down the deep mining operation at Nettleton and 48 men from Caistor and the surrounding area lost their jobs.

The miners' cottages were finally demolished around 1974, and the mine buildings dismantled. All the entrances were sealed but from time to time pit falls in the surrounding fields mark the presence of the underground tunnels.

THE STATUTE FAIRS

One tends to think that in the past no-one moved far from the village in which they were born, but the nineteenth century certainly saw a surprising amount of population movement as people followed opportunities for employment and/or housing. The 1851 Census reveals that 30 people born in South Kelsey were then living in nearby Nettleton, but by 1861 the number had dropped to 15 and by 1871 to 6. Quite a large proportion of those living in South Kelsey at that time had been born elsewhere, including the rector who came from Woolwich and his wife from Scotland.

April 6th, Lady Day, saw the waggoners with their families and belongings take to the road as they were hired by the year and could travel many miles to their next location. Similarly, farm labourers and their families were constantly on the move.

Some villagers today can remember that well into the middle of the century, April 6th was still known as "flitting day" when many of the farm labourers and their families would load their meagre belongings on to a horse drawn cart, leaving their tied cottage at the end of their annual contract to move to another farm for employment.

In Lincolnshire, the fourteenth of May used to be called "Pag Rag Day" when the unmarried farm workers and servant girls packed their few belongings and travelled to the nearest market town for the annual Hiring Fair in search of a new situation. They would then assemble in the market square, girls in one group, young men in another, their mode of dress or the tools they carried indicating their working skills. The farmers would then walk around inspecting them like so much cattle. On selection, a bargain would be struck by the acceptance of a shilling piece from his future employer, known as a "fastening penny" (a penny for each month of the year). This was the labourer's contract of employment for the year and no further wages would be forthcoming until the following Pag Rag Day. Occasionally, if he was a kindly man, the farmer would advance a few shillings in the autumn to enable the worker to buy warm winter clothing, but in any case, the year's wages would not amount to much more than £4. If a servant should ask for a rise at any time, the employer would often use this as an excuse to engage another, cheaper, servant in their place.

Workers from South Kelsey would travel either to Caistor, Market Rasen or Brigg, where the Statute Hirings drew hundreds from the surrounding areas, many agricultural workers and domestic and farm servants having to seek employment each year. Both masters and men would look forward to the outing for months determined to enjoy themselves. The farmers and their wives would stock up on farm provisions and the servants had to be content with more trivial purchases and the amusements afforded by the fairground booths paid from their newly acquired wages before making their way to their new positions.

In the 1850s and 1880s they were often denounced as immoral and drunken gatherings by the strict Methodist Temperance movement, but when the full impact of the agricultural depression began to be felt in the 70s and 80s the Statutes declined.

Although life must have been very hard, several dates in the annual calendar would have provided a welcome excuse for a break. Reports can be found of Annual Horse Races at Caistor (Feb/March 1819), annual Sheep Fairs at Caistor in April, the Nettleton Feast in October and Kelsey Feast and Moortown races (October 1870), not to mention the famous Brigg Horse Fairs.

AGRICULTURAL DEPRESSION

After the Land Enclosure Act that created a more efficient use of the land coupled with improved methods of farming, the new tenant farmers and landowners saw their profits rising and their standard of living vastly improved. But it did create an even sharper divide between them and the landless, vote-less and largely illiterate labourers who lived a precarious existence with no security of employment or home. The situation was further exacerbated at the end of the thirty years' war with France which saw 300,000 men suddenly thrown on the labour market causing mass unemployment and a general decline in trade, coupled with bad harvests in Britain in the years 1816-19. It took more than six years for the situation to improve, export trade increase and wheat prices to come down sufficiently for bread to come once more within the grasp of the poor.

As the nineteenth century rolled on, with the protection of the Corn Laws and little competition from abroad, British farming saw a "golden age" lasting about thirty years, when most of the food the population needed could be produced at home and sold at reasonable prices. Those workers who were employed on a full time basis on a farm were given a house and land to support themselves, but even this life could be threatened as the following example recorded in T.W.Beastall's "Agricultural Revolution in Lincolnshire", illustrates.

"Richard Hill was born at Waddingham in 1771 and married in 1802 at the age of 31. In 1808 he was employed as a waggoner by the Skipworth family in South Kelsey which entitled him to £10 a year, together with a house, garden, one rood of land and the keep of one cow and two pigs. The cow, fed on dried food in the crew-yard of his master's farm in the winter, was turned out to graze from the middle of April until November. Similarly, the two pigs would run in the fields from May to November and then brought in for the winter. After a few years on the farm, two farm servants were boarded with him and his wife for which they received for their upkeep a further £20 a year, another cow, two more pigs and the use of half-acre of potato ground . Richard and his wife lived on the farm in relative comfort until 1824, but ten years later at the age of 53, he was applying for poor relief for himself and three children at Hemswell-on-the-Clays."

During the eighteenth century landowners would often destroy cottages to avoid the cost of maintaining them and because too much accommodation in relation to employment meant higher poor rates. Labourers might only be employed for part of the year and then would be a charge on the Poor Relief. Only about one in five lived on the farms while the rest relied on daily or weekly contracts, severable at will, so that one third of the workforce was surplus to requirements. This created the formation of the gang system – gangs of labourers, many of them women and children (because they were cheaper) under the control of a gang master, that travelled from farm to farm in the most primitive conditions.

Then as Britain entered the 1870s, another agricultural depression began to bite. The vast corn growing areas of Lincolnshire and East Anglia were most hard hit, as cheap foreign imports from the newly opened up prairies of America brought the price of home-grown wheat tumbling down and the Government failed to step in with new Corn Laws as it had done after the Battle of Waterloo ended the war with France. The farm workers' wages were pitifully low and their living conditions quite often appalling. Many workers emigrated to the Colonies, no doubt lured by the tempting free passages offered and the glowing descriptions of the life abroad. However, a few letters filtered back describing the dreadful conditions aboard ship and often disappointing opportunities when they arrived.

Records do show that one Harry "Dab" Brooks, born in 1850 at Claxby married Susannah Skipworth, the daughter of George Borman Skipworth, at South Kelsey and then emigrated to Canada. They had five children and both parents died in Canada sometime in the early 1900s.

In 1874, after their employers refused to raise their wages, many farm labourers went on strike whereon the farmers retaliated by imposing a "lock-out". Others drifted into the towns and cities to take advantage of the opportunities and higher wages brought about by the Industrial Revolution. The Trade Union movement was emerging in the factories and in 1872 the Farm Workers' Union was formed, including a branch at South Kelsey but it was already in decline by 1885. As the President of the TUC was to say in 1894 "we are surrounded on all sides by agricultural labourers whose remoteness from each other makes their organisation very difficult and costly, while their low wages in villages and the ever spreading endeavours of farmers to grow crops without proper labour sends them into our towns to flood our markets, keep down wages and hinders the work of organisation." A newspaper report in November 1875 quotes – "Agricultural wages in the neighbourhood of Caistor for this week have been lowered to 2s. per day with only three days per week guaranteed. Farmers are absolutely unable to afford the labour they want and it is generally feared that wages will decline to 1/6d. per day before Christmas. The Caistor workhouse is already overcrowded."

On 9th November 1877 it was reported that at South Kelsey, George B. Skipworth had presided at a public Tea Meeting which replaced the traditional Harvest Home. He spoke saying that both Unions and farmers had their grievances, troubles and difficulties but he hoped that landlord, tenants and labourers would work together in peace as their interests were one. He seemed to have a surprising amount of sympathy for the labourers, despite being a farmer and landowner himself.

However, the rural crisis deepened and 1879 saw the blackest year yet in the country's history. Continued bad weather, costly overseas wars and overall rural trade depression had brought the farm labourer to his lowest ebb. As the bitter winter dragged on literally thousands were starving due to the severity of the weather. At Brigg, Market Rasen and Caistor, soup kitchens were set up to distribute food and coal to the destitute. In May 1885, the Lincolnshire Chronicle reporting on the Brigg Statute Fair that year said that waggoners were being paid £15-20 a year, ploughmen £12-15, lads £8-12, young boys £5-7 while women could expect up to £16 a year and girls £12.

As the century slowly entered the last decade conditions did little to improve and the farm worker continued to struggle for existence. Continued migration to the towns and emigration abroad would perhaps explain the marked decline in South Kelsey's population during that time.

THE POOR LAWS AND THE CAISTOR UNION

The first Poor Laws were introduced by Elizabeth I in 1601 to make the wealthier landowners responsible for the poor and destitute in their parish. Although sturdy beggars would be whipped as rogues or vagabonds, the infirm were granted licences allowing them to beg. Often such persons were relieved by the Church, and in 1590, a record appears in the South Kelsey Church accounts that 4d. was paid to a poor man and a lame lad and 20d. to maimed solders.

In 1782 an amended law was passed called Gilbert's Poor Law making the duty of looking after the helpless, aged and sick of all ages devolve upon the parish. It was to be administered by Parish overseers and financed out of a compulsory rate levied upon householders. The parish was also to provide work for the genuinely unemployed by supplying stocks of hemp and similar materials for them to work on. Those who might prefer the open road to this form of employment could be punished by the local justice of the peace as vagrants. The poor rate levy was often a subject of resentment from those who had to pay it and parish boundaries were strictly observed to ensure that no-one received poor relief should they stray in from another parish.

The Poor Law also stipulated that parishes might join together into "unions" to build poor houses for the aged and infirm poor. The purpose of these institutions was to transform paupers into self-reliant employees thus reducing the numbers of potential paupers in the future. At the same time, Sunday School teachers were exhorted to teach children not to become paupers by instilling in them the principles and disciplines of religious education at an early age. (See the Caistor Matrons' Society)

Thus in the first year of the nineteenth century William Dixon of Holton-le-Moor inspired the formation of the Caistor Society of Industry to serve the needs of 20 surrounding parishes. The House of Industry was built on nine acres of land donated by the Lord of the Manor and the freeholders of Caistor situated in an isolated position on Caistor Moor well away from the town and designed to deter the able-bodied from applying for Poor Relief and to humiliate those who did.   £2,500 was raised from the surrounding Parishes to furnish the building and offices and provide utensils and materials for employing the poor.

The 3-storey U-shaped building was one of the earliest workhouses to include a central hub from which the workhouse master could supervise the inmates' yards – males to the west and females to the east. It was completed around 1803 and housed at that time 24 adults and 18 children. The children were set to knitting and spinning woollen yarns and in 1820 it was reported that stocks of wool, yarns, flax, thread, etc., were maintained in the workhouse.

William Dixon was pleased to report in 1803 that the Society had restored "to the unclean poor, Cleanliness; to the drunken poor, Piety; and to the ignorant poor, Instruction". The views of the inmates were not recorded.

By 1816, a report claimed that the Workhouse was under-funded so parish contributions were raised. Each parish sending a pauper to the house had to pay 3/6d. per week per person, and the proportion of the pauper's earnings returned to the parish from whence he/she came was reduced.

After the Poor Law Amendment Act 1834, the care of the poor was put under the authority of a Board of Guardians, rather than individual parishes. The Caistor Society of Industry was dissolved and in November 1836 the New Caistor Union was formed to serve the needs of a total of seventy-six other parishes covering some 286 square miles thus becoming the largest such union in the country. This amalgamation only fostered more disputes as to the parish boundaries and who should take the responsibilities for "vagrants".

The Caistor Union Board of Guardians, of whom George Skipworth was a member used to meet each week at the Red Lion in Caistor to decide on the fate of all those who had made application for Poor Relief. Browsing through an abridged version of the Minutes of those meetings held between 1837 and 1848, the stark lists of people and the brief notes beside each name conjures up a picture of the miseries suffered by the poor at that time. The responsibility for each new person was closely studied and the cost for each applicant was assigned to the parish from which they came. Stringent efforts appear to have been made to return anyone who was not a resident of a parish covered by the Caistor Union. In 1837 there were three villagers from South Kelsey seeking assistance from the Workhouse, Thomas Spencer, Francis Drayton and Sarah Boughton and her 3-year-old child.

The Board of Guardians also appear to have been the forerunner of the present unpopular Child Support Agency, pursuing the fathers of illegitimate children and husbands who had deserted their wives and families and requiring them to provide support for their children rather than allowing them to become a burden on the parish. Women too were not encouraged to abandon their children. In 1841, the South Kelsey overseer was instructed to take steps against one Harriet Sherlock for deserting her children and leaving them to the parish and in 1845 Ann Whitehead deserted her two illegitimate children but when found again the next year refused to take them out of the workhouse. A ruling was also made that no unmarried pregnant woman would be accepted by the workhouse. The Board also took active steps to make adult children support their elderly parents rather than putting them into the workhouse.

Since reliance on the Poor Relief had become almost a way of life for the poorest workers, seeing it as the only way to supplement their pitifully low wages, the new law saw that conditions in the workhouse were made even more unattractive in an effort to discourage claimants. Families were separated, meals taken in silence and a host of petty rules imposed to add to their discomfort.

In addition the new law discouraged any parish relief to be given outside the workhouse, granting "out relief" only in certain circumstances such as to the very old or sick. Every week the Caistor Union's Relieving Officer toured the district assessing the eligibility of those claiming relief. Thus on Wednesday of each week, South Kelsey saw the arrival of the Officer, usually on foot, who had travelled from Normanby-le-Wold, via Claxby, Holton-le-Moor, to South Kelsey and then on to North Kelsey and Nettleton.

Conditions in the Workhouse were extremely harsh and the diet meagre – mainly bread, gruel and occasional cheese or poor quality meat. Inmates were set to picking oakum (unravelling old tarred ropes to be used as caulking for boats) and anyone absconding was severely punished, although one such runaway pleaded to be put back in prison as he said conditions were better there than the Workhouse. In March 1838 it was recorded that three men had absconded in order "to see a local steeplechase" while in another year three lads ran away but were quickly apprehended and returned to the workhouse. In 1837 an order was made for fastening the lower sashes of windows in the Women's Ward "to prevent the ingress and egress of paupers" though it might seem unlikely anyone would want to break in.

The state of the building can only be guessed at when one reads that the local ratcatcher was employed to fix grilles over the entrance to tunnels under the workhouse to prevent the entry of even more rats into the buildings.

Another indication of the harsh conditions within the workhouse emerges in 1843 with the note in the Minutes of a seven-year-old boy having had his finger amputated "following a blow from the schoolmaster".

In 1856 it is recorded that George Skipworth was Chairman of the Union Staff and the Board of Guardians was meeting every alternate Saturday at the Workhouse and in the 1886 election of Guardians, Mr. E. Walker of South Kelsey was sequestered for a year owing to the nominator not having paid his rates.

After the House of Industry was re-named the Workhouse, it also became responsible for the care of the insane but conditions were far from satisfactory. In 1835 one of the Guardians reported that of the three female lunatics held there, one was chained by her neck to the bedstead, while another had been confined to her bed for so long that her limbs were useless, but in her distress she tore off her clothes and was continually naked. Following another inspection revealing unacceptable conditions, a plea was made in 1836 for better treatment of the insane and this was to be done by removing them to a proper lunatic asylum. However, the 1881 Census of Residents reveals that thirteen people were still classified as imbeciles.

From this same Census listing a total of 174 people, only three were born at South Kelsey, a 60-year-old woman classified as an "imbecile", and two agricultural labourers aged 77 and 80 respectively. It is interesting to note that many of these agricultural labourers lived to a ripe old age, with ages ranging from 60 to 88 - a hard life maybe, but for some perhaps a relatively healthy one.

In 1929 the specially elected Board of Guardians was finally abolished as the Welfare State began to take over the old established Poor Law system, the concept of the Workhouse was phased out and by 1937 the building was listed as a certified Institution for the reception of mental defectives and contained 120 patients and re-named Caistor Hospital in 1938. It was finally closed down in July 1990 and the patients transferred to a purpose built unit at Immingham.

Over the years, an entrance block had been added (1837), a fever ward (1842), a school (1863-4), a chapel dedicated to St. Lawrence (1865) and an Infirmary was added in 1871. The Workhouse also had its own graveyard west of the chapel.

In January 2001 much of the main building was destroyed by fire leaving only the front block, Chapel and school block standing. The ruins still stand in neglected grounds off the Caistor road awaiting redevelopment.

In South Kelsey itself, almshouses were built in the field on the west side of the footpath and accessible down the side of Mill Farm. These were still owned by the Parish Council until the middle of the last century and were home to some of the village's elderly inhabitants until the last one died and the cottages were demolished.

FRIENDLY SOCIETIES

A Royal Foresters had been founded in Leeds in the 18th century mainly as a sociable society but gradually the members felt they had a duty to assist their fellow members who fell into need as "they walked through the forests of life".   This led to the foundation of The Ancient Order of Foresters in 1834.

The proliferation of so-called friendly societies in the latter half of the nineteenth century was brought on in no small measure by the adverse effects of the Poor Law Amendment Act.   Loosely based on the original club, the so-called Courts, consisting of elected members,   were responsible for their own funds and for the relief of their own members which was decided by democratic vote.

As the harshness of the Poor Law began to bite tradesmen, craftsmen and labourers in the neighbourhood of Caistor, Brigg and Binbrook came together to form a bond of brotherhood and friendship and provide their members with a minimum of financial security to protect them from the spectre of the workhouse and a pauper's grave.   Their monthly meetings, usually held in the local pub were a welcome social event and their annual processions and feasts became part of the village social life.

By 1871, it was reported that the South Kelsey Druids Society was celebrating its sixth anniversary with its members, accompanied by a band, processing round the village visiting the houses of neighbouring gentry and landowners who could usually be relied upon to make a contribution to their funds.   This was followed by a service at St. Mary's and a dinner at The Bull, which is where they held their normal monthly meetings.

In the same year they were joined by the Owersby Foresters who had previously met at the White Hart in North Owersby but which had been closed down that year. Half their 90 members then processed round their friends and patrons accompanied by the Market Rasen band before arriving at South Kelsey where they dined at The Bull. Two years later it was reported that the Owersby & South Kelsey Foresters' Friendly Society (mainly composed of journeymen farmers) were celebrating their annual festival in the usual style.   Mr. George B Skipworth of Moortown House presided at the dinner and wished the members well.

The friendly societies continued to flourish throughout the nineteenth century and club membership gave undoubted independence from the parish. The chance to be "on the club" rather than "on the parish" was an important source of pride to the working people. It did, however, still only cover a minority of the working population – the very poorest and women were still not represented and their plight was not to be addressed until the National Health Insurance Act of 1911 was put in place.

THE CAISTOR MATRON SOCIETY

The Caistor Matron Society was founded in 1808 by William Dixon of Holton-le-Moor as part of the educational experiments he had initiated at the Caistor Workhouse and was run by matrons of the local parishes. Its purpose was to foster and encourage the foundation and maintenance of Sunday Schools which it hoped children would attend from about the age of six until fourteen   The underlying object was to teach Christian principles to the children to ensure they grew up to become honest, hard-working and sober members of society (and not become a burden on the parish!).

On the annual July anniversary of the Society, Sunday School children from all the surrounding villages would be brought by wagon into Caistor. Here they formed a procession, each village carrying its individual flag and, accompanied by the Royal North Lincoln Militia band and the Caistor Juvenile Fife & Drum band, would march to Caistor Church for a sermon, after which books published by the Society for Promoting Christian Knowledge, would be distributed at the Matrons' own expense to "deserving children".   They would then assemble in the main square where refreshments would be set out and various stalls provided selling sweets and toys.   In the latter half of the century it was reported that refreshments had been provided for 850 children and the Anniversary Day continued to be held until just after the First World War.

SUNDAY SCHOOLS

A Sunday School was first set up by the Anglican Church in the village, until the Methodist movement started to offer strong competition. The chief aim was to give the children a grounding in Christian knowledge, but in the early days often provided the poorer children with the only access they had to a very basic education. For those children who were willing to learn, they could be taught at least to write their own name, and for the brighter ones a very elementary grasp of reading and writing. The classes would be taken by ladies in the village, and in South Kelsey the daughters of the squire, the Misses Skipworths, were known to help regularly at St. Mary's Sunday School.

By the middle of the nineteenth century, the children of the village were well-catered for by the several Sunday schools run by both St. Mary's and the three Methodist Chapels. One of the highlights of the year was the Chapel Anniversary Day held in July. Several weeks were spent in preparation for singing, reciting poems and for reading. Every child joined in and not a small part of the excitement were the new clothes bought specially for the occasion. All the Sunday schools combined that day and gathered in the Sunday School building on Caistor Road where a platform made it especially suitable for performances.

Sometimes a horse-drawn cart was pulled through the village carrying a band of singing children. Another exciting day for the children was the Annual Chapel Sunday School Outing when a charabanc was hired to transport the children for a day at Cleethorpes seaside.

During World War II, Church and Chapel combined their outings. No longer able to go to the seaside which was then all barricaded off for the duration, they would take a picnic lunch to Alkborough or Tealby. Yet another outing was the Caistor Matrons Society Day as described above.

THE METHODIST MOVEMENT

John Wesley was born in 1703 at the Epworth vicarage and went on to Oxford where he was ordained into the ministry. Whilst he was at Oxford he joined a group of serious minded students for regular prayer meetings and Bible readings which earned them the name of the Methodists. After leaving college he served in his father's parish at Epworth and for a while went as a missionary to the recently formed American colony of Georgia. Here he offended many by his arrogance as well as trying to impose stricter standards of conduct in the colonies. In 1738 he returned to England where in May of that year he underwent a conversion believing in the gospel of personal salvation by faith and convinced it was his duty to go out and teach others.

At no time did he have any desire to found a new church or sect and remained an Anglican throughout his life, but he received little or no support, and often outright hostility, from the traditional clergy. He did however have supporters although he and his fellow missionaries were often forced to preach in the open. Here he drew vast crowds and won converts by the hundreds from among the poorest of the population. His message offered new hope to the neglected workers giving them a self-respect and encouraging them to become hard-working, thrifty and sober, which by the latter years of the eighteenth century made them preferred employees. Although much of the Methodists' efforts were directed towards the poor of the cities and mining areas, their ideas would also appeal to the poorer members of the rural communities.

In 1791 John Wesley died and in the same year the new Methodist Church was formed and is today the largest English non-Conformist church in Britain. By 1815 there were a quarter of a million Wesleyan Methodists in England and Wales.

The new form of religious worship obviously appealed to the people of South Kelsey because by 1842 both the Wesleyans and the Primitive Methodists had built chapels here and by 1892 the Free Methodists had added another chapel together with a fourth at Moortown. A Sunday School was also built belonging to the United Methodist Chapel opposite, From Church Returns it can be seen that congregations at the Methodist Chapels were often as great as at St. Mary's.

In Victorian England the two religious groups, Anglican and non-Conformist, became very class divisive, the land owning classes clinging to the traditional Anglican church, and the working classes on the whole supporting the new non-conformist movement. Differences between "Church and Chapel" were very much part of village life. As late as the twentieth century a ballot taken to decide whether to ban games on the Recreation Ground on Sundays caused many of the old differences between the two to re-emerge.

All four chapels continued to attract congregations until after the end of World War II, when one by one they were sold off and converted into private dwellings. Only the Methodist chapel and schoolroom on the corner of the Brigg Road opposite the old Forge continues in active use.

EDUCATION

Long before it was made compulsory, the education of Kelsey children appears to have been the concern of the local gentry. It is thought the first Free School was erected around 1712 at the instigation of Lady Mary Ayscough, the widow of Sir Edward who had died in 1699, but was pulled down and rebuilt by Philip Skipworth soon after he bought the South Kelsey estate. At that time the schoolmaster was receiving a voluntary annuity of £18 from the estates. Returns to the Select Committee on the Education of the Poor, made by Thomas Wilby, curate, in 1818 recorded that 30 children were being instructed at his Lordship's expense in this new building   He did however remark that "many of the poor are without the means of education."

The school building was built on two floors and was the largest building in the village and lacking a Village Hall, the school room served many purposes. The Skipworth family as the school's benefactors frequently required the building. At half-yearly intervals the tenants' rents were collected there. Skipworth family gatherings used it for weddings and funerals because of its proximity to the Church (Moortown House was 2-1/2 miles away). Other organisations would use it for their meetings, and village concerts and like entertainments were held there.   In return for the use of their schoolroom, the children were given an annual treat by Mr. Skipworth who conveyed them to Moortown House by wagon where a sports day and refreshments were provided.

By 1835, 33 children were receiving free education with a further 16 paid for by their parents. The school now had a lending library attached. At the same time three other schools in the neighbourhood were providing education for some children of both sexes at their parents' expense. In 1850 around 60 children were attending Sunday School where they would have received the rudiments of reading and writing in addition to religious instruction.

From the Census taken in 1851 it can be seen that there were 143 children between the ages of 5-14, although less than half attended school Forster's Education Act passed in 1870 made education available, but not compulsory to all children. Controlled by locally elected School Boards, a network of elementary schools was formed but again attendance was neither compulsory nor free. Sandon's Act of 1876 and Mundella's Act of 1880 together made education compulsory to the age of 10 and in 1891 elementary education was made free. By 1899 the school leaving age was raised to 12 and in 1918 to 14.

In 1861 an adult education class was started for two hours three evenings a week to teach basic reading, writing and arithmetic skills, but this only lasted a couple of years. By the 1890's adult illiteracy had fallen dramatically and when adult classes were again started in 1895 they were in much broader subjects. However, poor attendance caused the classes to close in 1904.

Although a well respected member of the community, the schoolmaster was obliged to supplement his income. In 1842 George Tomlinson is recorded as "druggist and schoolmaster" whilst in 1847 William Lawrence, schoolmaster, was appointed Valuer to apportion rent charges in lieu of tithes It was also quite usual for the wife of the schoolmaster to act as an unpaid assistant and teach the younger children and instruct the older girls in needlework.

With the introduction of compulsory free education the status of the school teacher improved and upwards of three teachers would be employed at any one time. Monitors, boys of about 14, were also chosen from pupils attaining a certain standard to assist with teaching which helped to keep down costs. This system later developed into the pupil teacher system whereby boys and girls from 16-18 taught the younger children while at other times continuing their own education. This is logged after 1870.

Until 1880, when education was made compulsory to the age of 10, parents could withdraw their children at will and the school's Log Book records many occasions when school attendance was poor due to a farm sale or hunt, the potato planting and picking season and harvesting, and the despair of the teachers being unable to teach any new topic until after the October Feast (1866). A certain amount of bribery was sometimes employed by distributing sweetmeats to all children who attended school between harvest and Feast (Nov.1870).

Child labour included "tenting" – keeping an eye on beasts grazing the roadside verges – "turniping sheep" – trimming turnips before putting them through the turnip cutter to be fed twice daily to sheep , "potato setting", gleaning and picking twitch – weeding fields.

Illness caused much of the absenteeism – ringworm was highly contagious and extremely prevalent in farming communities, while whooping cough, scarlet fever, mumps, smallpox and chilblains were all common ailments.

Throughout the nineteenth century the increasing availability of education for the poorer children was usually welcomed by their parents, unless it interfered with their ability to contribute to the family's finances. Several families objected to their children being given homework, even when the pupils themselves were willing. When parents' inability to find the few pence necessary for their children to attend caused absenteeism more deserving children were sometimes subsidised by wealthier members of the community.

For several years, however, the Martin family living at Sunshine Farm, posed a constant challenge to the school master. In 1877, Mary Martin threatened to take the school master, Mr. Statham, to court, if he continued to punish her daughter Amelia for talking in class. She also objected strongly to her son Henry being caned for continually coming to school dirty. It seems that parents threatening school teachers is not a modern phenomenon. In 1882, tired of the continual invasion of children, animals and fowl from the Martin's land which adjoined his, Mr Statham had his backyard fenced in. This so incensed Mr. Martin that he stopped paying the school fees for his son, George, who was in turn sent home. This culminated in Mr Martin appearing in court and being fined. In 1883 he was again in court for his daughter's bad attendance.

In 1878 the school building was restored to provide places for 120 children, but an average attendance in 1892 was 70. In 1906 it was again pulled down and rebuilt.

In the latter half of the 19th century not only the three Rs were taught but also instruction in carpentry and gardening were included in the curriculum, and in the early 20th century pupils were tending a flourishing garden in the school grounds.

An ex-Mayor of Lincoln, John Mills, was a pupil here and his portrait used to hang in pride of place in the school.

There are still people living in the village who remember going to the old school, but in July 1974 it was closed down and the village children are now bussed to North Kelsey Primary and other schools in the area. The Old School, complete with the adjoining Headmaster's house, is situated on the cross roads opposite the Church and scheduled as a Grade II Listed Building.

VILLAGE LIFE IN THE NINETEENTH CENTURY

From 1793-1815, Great Britain was almost continuously at war with France and the strain on Britain's economy was greater than ever before while the morale of her people was severely taxed. The war did however stimulate the agricultural industry and farmers were encouraged to put more land under the plough. New farming techniques were introduced to increase productivity of the land and this all enabled Britain to supply the majority of her own food despite French blockades and severe restrictions on import trade. But the population was rising fast and there were soldiers, both British and Allied, to feed, transport was bad causing serious local grain shortages, wheat prices rose sharply and food prices in general increased. Despite all this, farmers did well on the high prices, though seldom passing them on in higher wages for their labourers. While in the thirty years prices nearly doubled, the farm workers' wages rose scarcely at all and they suffered real distress.

The war also caused a drain on manpower - local men were liable to serve in the militia and no doubt the recruiting officials visited South Kelsey during the late 18th century to try and enlist men for the army. They were not always welcome and in 1796 recruiting officials were opposed by a mob in nearby Caistor who burnt the returns listing men's names thus provoking the quartering of soldiers in surrounding towns. It should be noted, however, that the Lincolnshire Legion of Volunteers was formed at this time and many a starving farm labourer might have seen army life as preferable to that of hopeless destitution on the land.

All the events in the outer world would have had some effect on the small villages of Lincolnshire but the industrial revolution which was sweeping many parts of the country throughout the nineteenth century seems to have passed South Kelsey by and it continued to be almost entirely reliant on agriculture.

The one greatest factor affecting the villagers' lives was the Land Enclosure Act. This had deprived many of them of their strip of land and the right to graze animals on common land and they became totally dependent on their ability to find work. Fortunately the Skipworth family, unlike many of the landed gentry in those days, appear to have felt a responsibility and sympathy for their workers and were a benevolent influence on the village. The bulk of the land here was still owned by the

Lord of the Manor and most of the villagers lived in farmhouses or tied cottages, there were few yeoman farmers, which enabled them to grow a certain amount of food in their own gardens. This could include cabbages, carrots, peas and beans, leeks and onions, turnips and swedes, parsnips and potatoes, and a uniquely Lincolnshire crop – Mercury or markberry, a spring perennial tasting much like spinach.

Of necessity, most farm work could only be carried out during the hours of daylight, and firewood, and even dried cow pats, could be collected from the local woods and fields to give warmth during the winter months. Only if they lost their "tied" cottage or illness or old age prevented them from working did the threat of the workhouse loom. It was these circumstances that saw the rise of the Friendly societies and South Kelsey had its own Druids Lodge of Foresters (see page 80).

But although life was still hard and more so if the crops failed when the farm labourer could still become destitute and his family go hungry, his lot was probably fractionally better than for those who had migrated to the cities and were crowded into cramped, squalid living accommodation where disease was always present, and working long hours in dangerous conditions for a pittance.

Even with the loss of common land for pasturage, keeping a cow could still be part of a tied labourer's terms of employment. The cow would be turned out on to the employer's pasture or allowed to graze along the highways. The milk produced was an important part of the labourer's diet, forming the basis of almost daily milk puddings, cheese and butter, and buttermilk for feeding the pigs.

A newly calved cow produces colostrum – better known in this part of the world as "beastlings" or "bezzlings", for several days before the true milk comes through. This is quite unlike milk and unsuitable for making into butter or cheese, but is very rich and makes particularly good custards and puddings. As large quantities were usually produced it was often taken in jugfuls round to friends and neighbours and tradition dictated that the jug should be returned unwashed otherwise the cow would run dry.

If there were any surplus bull calves these would be slaughtered to provide the family with welcome fresh meat. This event often coincided with Easter and some of the meat was reserved for celebrating Easter Sunday.

Pigs were also a staple part of the villagers' diet and nearly every household had a pigsty in their gardens, a tradition which went on well into the middle of the twentieth century. The pigs were nearly always killed during the winter months when the colder weather ruled out the possibilities of contamination due to flies and warmth. The whole process could take several days – after fasting overnight, the pig had its throat cut and as much blood as possible was forced out of its jugular vein. It would then be placed in a scalding tub where near boiling water was poured over it and the hair and scurf was scraped off the whole body. After chilling, the head and trotters were cut off and the carcass suspended on a tripod while its innards were removed. Every part of the pig was utilised for food, not a scrap being wasted. Much of the meat was made into fat bacon which for many decades formed a staple food being eaten every day while the women folk made brawn, haslets, sausages and pies from the offal, as well as preparing the typical Lincolnshire dish of stuffed chine. Although the task of slaughtering and butchering was taken over by one man touring the village in later years, some villagers can still remember the days of "putting away the pig".

The 1832 Reform Act gave the franchise to so-called "£10 householders" thereby increasing the number of South Kelsey voters from 6 in 1832 to 17 in 1838, but true democracy did not reach the rural areas until almost the turn of the century.

Some idea of the make-up of the village's population can be gleaned from the 1851 Census. Of the 621 inhabitants listed, 86 were children under 4, 143 were of school age i.e. 5-14 (although it is noted elsewhere that less than half attended fulltime education), 240 were aged between 15 and 64 (reasonable working age) the rest were aged over 65. Of the male population 137 men and boys (from the age of 11) were employed in agriculture and another 69 in miscellaneous trades and crafts. 54 women in paid work were mainly in domestic service, although one or two were shopkeepers or dressmakers. Weaving had also been an important cottage industry and the Lincolnshire Chronicle reported that at the turn of the century (1800) 17 weavers and their families plied their trade in South Kelsey but by 1859 only John Brown still had one working loom.

1856 White's Directory described South Kelsey as a pleasant scattered village of some 632 souls and 4980 acres of land, including the hamlet of Moortown, or Riverhead as it was sometimes called. In 1881 the population was 615, in 1871 – 633, in 1891 – 583, but by 1921 had dropped to 502. In 1981 the figure was as low as 449 (identical to that in 1801) while the present number is increasing rapidly as more new houses are built.

In September 1859, the Lincolnshire Chronicle reported on an incident at the Skipworth Arms. Two publicans, one known as the Roaring Lion, got very drunk and proceeded to break nearly all the glass and earthenware in the house. They then started to fight through one of the windows, breaking nine or ten panes of glass in the process, until one of them had to stop because he had nearly severed his thumb and had badly cut his wrist on the broken glass. Despite the relative seriousness of the affair the Market Rasen police were not called out and the combatants escaped punishment. Maybe it was because of such incidents that the inhabitants of Kelsey earned the criticism in the Stamford Mercury in 1872 that they were "dirty, drunken and disreputable". In reply, "An Old Ratepayer" immediately sprang to their defence and described them as "The genuine Kelseian is a stout, robust, fun-loving fellow, rather noisy sometimes, hence he is sometimes called a tippler, but he is generally a good neighbour and loves to associate with his fellows and laugh".

One of the most far reaching changes that came about in the nineteenth century was the growth of education. In 1800 voluntary education had been provided by the Skipworth's School and the Sunday schools, but by the end of the century the National School made free education compulsory for all children under the age of 12. This created a literate workforce and greatly reduced the amount of cheap child labour in the fields.

FROM 1900 TO THE PRESENT DAY

As the village entered the 20th century it still remained a mainly rural community. Most of the population were still engaged in agriculture, either as self employed farmers or agricultural workers. At the same time, the village was still almost completely self-supporting and most trades were represented living in the village – carriers, butcher, wheelwright, miller and baker, plumber, bricklayers, and builder, boot and shoe maker, saddler, rope maker, carpenter, blacksmith and agricultural machine and implement maker, grocer and draper, shopkeeper, dressmaker and tailor.

The villagers' diet was still pretty simple, based mainly on what was available locally. Rabbits, which had become scarce in the 19th century due to the decline in the rabbit fur market, were now more plentiful and no longer regarded as farmed animals and therefore not illegal to trap providing a cheap source of meat along with pigs and their products. Hedgehogs were sometimes baked in clay and squirrel pie would have been eaten by some. In the 1900s pigeon pie (breasts layered with bacon) and starling breasts braised in cider with bacon, were an occasional delicacy. Hedgerow fruits and nuts continued to be harvested and preserved for the winter while the cottage garden provided vegetables.

South Kelsey was the birthplace of Lincolnshire's first airman. Montague F Glew was born at Hall Farm in 1893, the second son of Walter Glew and nephew of John G Glew, MP of Market Rasen The family later moved to a farm at Wittering, Northants, from where he went to Blackburn Flying School at Hendon and obtained his flying licence No. 410 on 4th February 1913. He then purchased a D type Blackburn monoplane from Cyril Foggin, whose youngest sister, incidentally, he married in 1922.

On 12th July, 1913, the Lincolnshire Life magazine contained a lengthy report on the first Aircraft Flying Display to be held in Lincolnshire in Mr.Blakey's field off the Legsby Road. Flying his recently purchased Blackburn monoplane built in 1912, boasting 50 h.p. and a top speed of 60 m.p.h. in ideal conditions, Montague F. Glew, then aged 20, gave various displays of flying and made several trips before engine failure caused him to crash land on a ploughed field damaging the plane but escaping himself without injury. Onlookers took the opportunity to collect splinters of the wooden propeller and the aviator obligingly autographed them as souvenirs. The plane was repaired and later flew at Horncastle where it crashed again but without injuring the pilot. After another crash in 1914 the plane was stored at the Glews' Wittering farm where it was later discovered in 1937 and taken to the Shuttleworth Museum at Old Warden, Biggleswade, Beds, where it can still be seen as the oldest British built aeroplane in the world still capable of flight. Montague Glew died in 1969 at Market Harborough.

Montague's eldest brother, Aubrey Edmond Glew, joined the Lincolnshire Yeomanry in 1914 seeing action as a despatch rider before transferring to the Royal Flying Corps and getting his wings in May 1916. He was a second lieutenant with 24 Sqn. RFC for two brief months before being killed over German lines on 8th September 1916. He had shot down four German planes. His grave is at St. Pierre, Amiens, France but his memorial, one of very few RFC monuments in the country, can be seen in St. Nicholas Churchyard, South Kelsey. He is also remembered on the Roll of Honour at Stamford School where he had been a pupil and on the War Memorial at Wittering. Ironically, Montague was unable to fly during the Great War as he was found to be too short sighted.

When World War I was declared the young men from every village spurred on by patriotic fervour hurried to enlist, but nine would never return to South Kelsey and others would be wounded. One man employed as a road sweeper, or lengthsman as they were called, had lost all his toes to frostbite while serving in the trenches.

German Zeppelins often passed overhead, following railway lines and the River Humber on their way to attack inland cities, and on returning would dump unused bombs and empty petrol tanks to help increase their speed across the North Sea and to escape being intercepted by British planes from Elsham, Killingham and other stations. One such tank fell and exploded on the drive of Holton Park.

Between the Wars the village continued to be very much self-sufficient with a tremendous sense of community - most daily needs were catered for and entertainment provided within the parish. Money would always have been scarce in this rural community and many times no money would change hands when goods were exchanged by bartering. There were however five village shops, a butcher, two boot repairers (everyone wore leather soled boots in those days) three joiners' shops, a tinsmith, a fish shop that fried several times a week, and at that time one could still purchase bread from the Old Bakery by the side of Mill Farm.

Milk was produced by local dairy herds and delivered around the area by pony and trap. One such was Kelsey House farm. The cows were milked in the shed attached to the granary and delivered on alternate days as far as Thornton-le-Moor and Moortown by the sons of the house before they went to school and again after they came home in the afternoon. Mount Pleasant farm in North End Lane also supplied milk locally, including filling the one-third pint bottles and supplying them to the school. It may be remembered that at one time all schoolchildren were provided with free milk each day. There was no Milk Marketing Board and EEC in those days with which to contend.

Samuel and Louise Fosten ran a thriving tailor and dressmaking business at Keptie House (now the Abacus Playgroup). Along the Caistor Road, a thatched hardware shop sold paraffin, etc. while the Martins at Sunshine Farm sold coal and hired out horses during the summer to Lincolnshire County Council to pull tar pots on the roads. There was also a small butcher's shop on the side of the house (it is still possible to see the bricked up entrance in the wall) with a slaughterhouse in the back yard.

The Baldersons opened their general store on the crossroads in 1932, finally closing in 1989. The Kirkby Shop (now Church View) kept 3 people fully employed. Next door to the Blacksmith's shop on the Brigg Road Jack Staves had a Bike Shop, both of which employed several people, while Dannatt's Joinery Shop opposite also employed several men and boys.

Few people owned private cars in those early days, one was the Vicar with a Singer and another belonged to Mr. Hardy at Melrose, while several tradesmen ran motor delivery vans. However, there were buses running through the village on a regular basis and trains would stop at each signal station.

Between the wars and for a short time after, the annual South Kelsey Show and Flower Show were held on a Wednesday in July each summer in the large field behind Melrose House. The school children were given a half day off and all the villagers took part. It was a time when horses were still very much a part of the countryside scene and there was tremendous rivalry among the waggoners for their horses to be judged best of Show. All types of horses would have been specially groomed ready for the parade along the village street.

Another annual event was the South Kelsey Feast – this was held on the last Sunday in October when a travelling fair would arrive in the village and set up its stalls and sideshows around the crossroads and in the pub yard.

During and just after World War II, villagers would congregate at the Kelsey House granary where the first floor store would be cleared and a temporary partition erected at the end behind which refreshments were prepared on a primus stove. For 1s.6d. they would play twelve hands of whist, then be served teas through the hatch in the partition, followed by dancing for the rest of the evening. Music was provided by Betty Crosby on the piano.

Other forms of local entertainment were the garden fetes, dances, whist drives and choir concerts often used as a way of raising funds for the Church and Chapels, and always receiving a lot of support. At that time, both Church and Chapels were well-attended providing a social meeting point for the villagers.

Before the days of universal immunisation, epidemics of childhood diseases, would occasionally sweep through the village with often tragic results. One such was in 1938, when scarlet fever raged for nearly a year, affecting almost every family in the community and putting many children into the nearby Osgodby Hospital for several weeks of recuperation.

As the village entered the third decade, the local roads were hard surfaced making travel between the villages much easier, and pavements and kerbs were being laid in the village itself. Until this time water came only from public and private wells and there were at least four parish pumps in the village, but in 1937-38 mains water and sewerage were connected to the village together with mains electricity and the telephone service. Street lighting was not installed, however, until 1960.

In 1937, on Monday 25th October, a freak whirlwind hit the area causing a considerable amount of damage and alarm, though fortunately no-one was injured. The storm appears to have been only a few yards wide and at its fiercest stretched for some three miles, embracing South and North Kelsey. Dozens of trees were uprooted and flung yards away, chicken houses were lifted up and carried considerable distances leaving their terrified occupants scattered around the fields or vanished forever. Most of the houses at the north end of the village lost their roofs and the village joinery shop belonging to Mr. H. Dannatt and Mr. G. E. Blackburn's blacksmiths were severely damaged.

One villager recalls how, as a small boy he watched from the schoolroom window as almost all the sycamore trees surrounding St. Mary's church were completely destroyed. Everyone had their own remarkable tale to tell.

With the outbreak of war in 1939, the outside world broke into the rural peace of the village. Once again the young men enlisted into the armed forces, apart from those considered essential to food production, and more women and girls went to work on the land. Ration books were issued in 1939 and the rationing of foodstuffs was phased in during 1940. Strange new foods appeared on the shelves – saccharine, Koo jam, tuna, whale meat, dried eggs and potatoes and everyone was encouraged to grow as much of their own food as possible. "Dig for Victory" was the motto as flower gardens gave way to vegetable plots.

For generations, nearly every household had a pigsty which housed a pig, fed on kitchen scraps providing much of the family's meat supply for the year. The pig would most probably have been the Curly Coat variety, a breed unique to Lincolnshire, a large hardy animal some 30 stone in weight consisting of a large proportion of fat suitable for the bacon which was produced in large quantities. This pig continued to be popular until in 1972 it became extinct in this country. However, in the 1920s many had been exported to Hungary where they had been crossed with a local breed and the Curly Coat was reintroduced to Britain in 2007. During the war villagers were encouraged to continue the practice and a strict control was kept on the number of pigs per household. Once a year someone would come round and slaughter the pigs on site after which they would be hung on beams in the cellar or on tripods outside to drain before being taken away for butchering. Up until the beginning of the war at least, every pig owner contributed a few pence each week to the Pig Club which could be drawn upon should there be an unforeseen expense, such as vet's fees, or even to replace the pig itself should it die.

Traditional skills were still being practised – one farmer's wife remembers her mother churning butter and lowering it down their well to keep cool. Surplus butter, and eggs, would be taken to the local shop to be sold.

Clothes rationing was introduced in June 1942 and make do and mend became another necessity. The same year saw petrol for private motorists become unavailable and pink "commercial" petrol was introduced to counter illegal use. Petrol rationing continued until the mid 1950s, long after the war had ended.

Several evacuees from Leeds were billeted in the village and one at least stayed on after the War, married, and settled locally. They attended the village school and when the occasional air raid siren sounded trooped with the other children across the road to the large cellar under the Bull Inn which served the school as an air-raid shelter.

Fifty or more years ago, the winters were on the whole much colder than today, and most years the field opposite Manor Farm, where now stand five modern bungalows, would flood and freeze over as did the pond beside Manor Farm, providing a skating rink for the local children giving them a welcome change of recreation.

For the men left behind, the 7th Lindsey Battalion of the Home Guard was formed, covering a large area including Brocklesby, Swallow, Rothwell, Holton-le-Moor, North and South Kelsey, Ownby, Clixby, Searsby, Great Limber and Grasby. Their commander was Joseph Nickerson (later Sir Joseph Nickerson of Rothwell) who said "we want in the villages and on isolated farms a body of men ready to deal with paratroopers in any sudden surprise attack. We want men who are able to kill and move unseen in the countryside they know so well".

The South Kelsey branch, under the command of Capt. D.S.Parker of Caistor, was known as Patrol 2A and consisted of Patrol Leader, Sgt. G. Blackburn, Cpl. J. Markham, and Pte's C. Everatt, H. Foster, and J. A. Constable.

A curious relic of the War, described in a book called "The Secret Army", survives on the south bank of the canal just below Moor Lock. An inconspicuous mound of earth sheltered by a small coppice conceals a World War II "Auxiliary Hide". These were used by special Auxiliary Units of the Home Guard. Formed in 1940, members of this highly secret underground resistance organisation were trained in sabotage and assassination In the event of invasion the units were to go to ground in the hides, to emerge behind enemy lines to carry out sabotage operations each unit operating independently and in secret. The location of only three are known in this county. The organisation was finally stood down in 1944 but has never been officially recognised. The present farmer obviously did know of its existence and the hideout has been used as a game rearing shelter, approached by a narrow bridge over the canal.

Although occasionally a stray German bomber would fly overhead – one flew up the Ancholme and off-loaded its bombs on Brandy Wharf and the yard at Holm Hill farm, destroying pig sties and killing a number of pigs – their main targets were Grimsby, Hull and inland cities. Hull's docklands suffered severely from incendiary attack and villagers could see from their upstairs windows the red glow in the sky and on one occasion pieces of burnt paper floated down like black snow.

South Kelsey was of course in the middle of Bomber County and many nights would see and hear a thousand British bombers flying over to raid targets in Germany. Heavy bombers were based at Hemswell, Scampton, Skellingthorpe, Waddington and Faldingworth, while fighter planes were stationed at Kirton Lindsey and Hibalstow.

After the war, there were still several shops in the village, Kirkby's grocer at Church View, Mrs.Balderson's store at the crossroads, the original Post Office and store opposite the Village Hall, a fish shop two houses down from the Methodist Chapel, and a petrol filling station at the Forge workshop and Balderson's garage, but one by one they closed down until none were left, like so many rural communities these days.

At the same time most of the resident tradespeople disappeared and the number of farm workers dramatically dwindled. The village was no longer a self-contained, self-sufficient community as farms became more and more mechanised, transport improved and the younger generation looked outside the village for employment.

One trade which had adapted to the modern world was the forge which after the war had evolved into an agricultural machinery workshop, but this again was closed down towards the end of the century. The owners of this business were the Blackburns and a few moments must be spared here to tell the story of Mrs Blackburn's uncle who came to live with them in the 1960s.

Reg May had not been born in South Kelsey, he had lived and worked in the area around Limber until he retired. All that time he had kept detailed diaries and made amateur nature films of the wildlife he had observed as a schoolboy and during his career as the local postman and farm worker. His finest hour as an ornithologist came in 1947 when he correctly identified the first sighting of the collared dove in the wild in Britain, despite the initial scepticism of the experts. He never married and when he came to South Kelsey to live with his niece at Forge Farm he managed to persuade the owners of Jarvis Plantation, an area of some 3 acres of woodland alongside the Canal, to let him make it a nature reserve. He cut back the trees and cleared some of the bushes which encouraged wild flowers and butterflies while birds and animals thrived there. He was 65 and for the next twenty years he became a familiar sight driving round in his old Morris Minor shooting brake. Sometimes he could be found perched up in a tree observing badgers and at others taking yet more films of the wild life, but age began to take its toll. In 1989 his story caught the imagination of the Binbrook-based Praxis Films Ltd. and a half-hour programme called Reg's Kingdom was broadcast by Yorkshire

Television.   He was passionate about the countryside and worried to the end that modern farming methods would damage the wildlife beyond redemption.

In 1990, the villagers all gathered in the Village Hall in a united effort to fight a proposal from Unigate to build a "chicken factory farm" on land near Gypsy Lane. They planned to build ten large sheds to house 400,000 chickens at any one time, a farm manager's bungalow, a generator and a substation. If built it was estimated that it would generate 4,000 tonnes of manure a year, the inevitable smell, the need for 6,000 gallons of water a day from an already overstretched supply and possibly 400 heavy lorry journeys each week on an inadequate network of narrow country roads. The village voted unanimously to reject the proposal and the planning application was turned down on environmental grounds by the Council later that year.

The post-war years saw various clubs forming in the village, a Women's Institute (since closed down), Kelsey Wives Group, a Luncheon Club, and the Monday Club. There is also a Gardening Club, an Indoor Bowls group and a Youth Club. These are variously housed in the Methodist Schoolroom and the Village Hall.

SOUTH KELSEY CLOSE – THE VILLAGE PLAYGROUND

Visitors to the Church may have remarked on the plaque commemorating the gift of a playground to the residents of South Kelsey and the story behind this gift is worth telling.

George Skipworth married Amelia Margaretta (Emily) Dixon of Holton Hall on 9th March 1815 and moved into Moortown House. In the years between 1816 and 1835 they had thirteen children, eight sons and five daughters. Sadly, all but one son died, and four of the five daughters married in St. Mary's Church before moving away.

Rosamund Frances (Fanny) Skipworth was born on 21st November 1823, being the sixth child and second daughter of the Skipworths. She and her sisters taught at the Sunday school, leaving home every Sunday morning and having lunch in the village. Despite several offers of marriage, Miss Fanny preferred her independence and stayed at home to help her father in his business and was a great comfort to her parents as one by one her brothers died, some in the prime of life. On 21st December 1859 her father, George, died and the house and estates became the property of his remaining son, George Borman Skipworth.

His widow, accompanied by Fanny, moved to Risley Hall, Derbyshire, which had been bought by her son-in-law, John Ffytche. It was a beautiful house and here she lived for the rest of her life, frequently visited by her daughters and their families and always hosted huge family gatherings at Christmas. Fanny continued her work with the Church and for the good of the village. At the age of 85, Mrs. Skipworth died and her ashes were brought back to South Kelsey churchyard.

Leaving Risley Hall, Fanny Skipworth rented a property in London, 16 Granville Place, and continued to hold open house for her sisters, provided the funds to renovate St. Mary's, at the same time being a devoted aunt to her many nephews and nieces. She took a particular interest in her godson, Edward James Gibbons, a barrister in London, and was planning to leave much of her fortune to him, but he died on the way to serve in the South African War and was buried at sea. It is said she never quite got over his death. Miss Fanny died on 30th August 1908 and was buried in the family vault at St. Mary's. At the large gathering at her funeral, former Sunday School pupils carried her coffin to its last resting place.

In gratitude for all her work for the community, it was felt a fitting memorial should be provided. A stained glass window was first considered but, at the suggestion of the Rev. Dixon of Holton Hall one of Fanny's numerous nephews and great nephews it was decided that, because of her lifelong love and care of children, a piece of land should be purchased and given to the parish as a permanent playground for the residents. Nineteen members of Fanny's family contributed £150 towards the purchase and the donor of the land offered to provide a fence, complete with gates. The playground officially opened on 18th June 1922 and a tea party was provided in the schoolroom by the ladies of the village. The Rev. Dixon made a speech and George P. Skipworth and his brother Lionel, declared the ground open.

For many years thriving football and cricket clubs used the playing field for practice and to hold matches against rival village teams, but sadly in 1997 vandals destroyed the clubhouse and the teams had to find alternative grounds and were both lost to the village.

There was also a grass tennis court and a bowling green situated at the top end of the field all now vanished. In the 1930s the ground provided the venue for the popular Summer Fetes run by the various village sports clubs.

1973 marked Conservation Year and the children of South Kelsey School raised funds to provide and plant 36 trees around the field and another tree was planted by the Parish Council to mark the Millenium.

In 2007, plans were being made to incorporate the field between the recreation ground and the Village Hall into one much larger area for the villagers' use.

THE VILLAGE SPORTS CLUBS

A flourishing cricket club had been formed sometime in the first half of the 20th century, playing on the recreation ground. The team played all the local teams and under Walt Blackburn was the first team to gain promotion to the Lincolnshire League 1st Division in 1984. Walt Blackburn, who lived in Skipworth Ridge overlooking the cricket ground, first played as a schoolboy of 13 and stayed with the team for 50 years. He was captain for 14 years and later Secretary for many years. He and his friend Ashley Cooper were friends of Freddie Trueman, the famous Yorkshire cricketer, who, when he was stationed at RAF Hemswell, signed on for South Kelsey but seldom actually played as he was frequently called upon to represent the RAF, but on one memorable occasion it was said he took 10 wickets for 11 runs against Caistor!

Freddie was a frequent visitor to the village and in 1952 was asked to present the awards at the end of season get-together. He agreed to do so but then found he had a 48-hour pass for that weekend. When Walt heard this he contacted the base commanding officer and had the pass cancelled. Thus one foggy autumn night, a very irate fast bowler was picked up from the station and taken to the Red Lion at Caistor to present the cups. His comments made at the time were not recorded!

During the War Major Wright, the headmaster of South Kelsey School, ran a Kelsey XI made up of guests and some villagers, including John Parkinson Snr of Church Farm. They played against Forces teams from KirtonHemswell, Scampton, Elsham and Binbrook and in 1945 took over the RAF Caistor fixtures and played against Australians based at Binbrook and West Indians at Hibaldstow. In 1947 Kelsey joined the Scunthorpe and District League but soon switched to Grimsby League. In 1953 they got to the finals of the Grimsby KO Cup but did not win. In 1952 Ted Sparrow made 92 not out in a score of 267 against Fisons, which was the team's highest total to date. At that time the team had a promising crop of young teenagers. The last game was played at South Kelsey in 1997 although the Kelsey team still plays elsewhere after their clubhouse burnt down around that time.

On 2nd August 1922, a group of villagers met to discuss the formation of a South Kelsey Football Club. Among the first officers of the club were J Chambers who took on the duties of secretary and held the post until

1935, and J. Markham who was elected Captain. A subscription of three shillings was agreed and red and white shirts, nets and two footballs were to be purchased. They would play on the village recreation ground beyond the tennis court situated beside the road. By the spring of 1923 the new team had already played several matches with neighbouring villages and had joined the Market Rasen Villages League and sometime later the West Wolds League During the summer of 1923 a garden fete had been held to raise funds and a dinner was arranged for the autumn. By this time a ladies committee had been formed to handle the catering for social events.

Familiar local names appear again and again in the Club's Minutes Book such as Barr, Blackburn, Dawson, Foston, Martin, Mumby, Parkinson and the Rev. Ireland. For some time Balderson's bus was used to transport players to away matches and later the bus from Caistor. One regular fixture before the War appears to be a friendly at-home match with North Kelsey on Christmas morning followed by a return away match on Boxing Day. Another match was with the Grimsby Police team on Good Friday.

In 1925 the Parish Council offered £1 towards the cost of providing a lavatory on the recreation ground and both the Tennis and Bowls Clubs were asked to contribute but no further mention is made in the minutes. In 1936, a groundsman was employed to prepare the pitch for a shilling a match. Committee meetings continued to be held on a very regular basis usually in the schoolroom, either to select the team for forthcoming matches or to make arrangements for fund raising events which included garden parties and fetes, dinners and socials, whist drives and concerts and in the years leading up to 1939, meetings were being held every week at The Bull.

A description of the summer fete in 1935 included a fancy dress parade for both children and adults, hoop-la, skittles, bowls, treasure hunt, egg & spoon race, tug-of-war and other ingenious games. The ladies committee agreed to run an ice cream stall and the local shops were asked whether they would like to rent a stall to sell their goods. A tennis tournament was also held at the same time utilising the Club's own court on the recreation ground, together with those in the village kindly loaned by Messrs. Hardy, Barr and Harrison.

By the end of 1939, after the outbreak of war, the football club appears to have been disbanded but was reformed for the 1946-47 season. In living memory there was also a ladies' football club for a short time. The finals of the West Wold League were held on the South Kelsey pitch on more than one occasion. The Club continued to thrive during the post war years, sharing the cricket club's pavilion but when this was destroyed by vandals in 1997 the two clubs had to find alternative accommodation and were both lost to the village.

A grass tennis court used to occupy the top end of the recreation ground and a Club team, captained after the War by John Husband, played other teams in the area. It was in existence in the 1920's and closed sometime in the 70's, but all evidence of it has now disappeared.

The small hut which provided storage facilities for the club was donated by the Barratts who lived opposite Manor Farm and used the hut beside their house as a small grocer's shop. When the shop closed the hut was dismantled and re-erected on the recreation ground.

THE VILLAGE HALL

After the first World War, John Hardy, JP, who was then living in Melrose House, bought a couple of old army huts and placed them on what is now the Village Hall site to provide rent-free accommodation for his retired farm workers. After they had been vacated, in December 1950, 0.186 acres of land was sold by the Parish Council for the sum of £40 and the old army huts were bought by the villagers in 1953 and converted into a Village Hall.

The idea of a Village Hall first emerged during the War, when in 1942 a War effort in the school playground raised £142 which was placed into War Bonds. At that time it was decided the money should go towards a permanent Village Hall. Little by little the original sum snowballed and advantage was taken to achieve that ambition when the opportunity arose to obtain a site and purchase a suitable building. Previously, dances, whist drives and socials had been held in the school house and the first floor room of the granary belonging to Kelsey House farm in the middle of the village.

In 1953 the opening ceremony was performed by Capt. Cruikshank, MP for Gainsborough and the hall was well-used for the next twenty years. However, the building eventually started to decay and the villagers formed a committee to raise money for a new building. South Kelsey had a strong sense of community and villagers worked together for three years raising £4,000 towards the new building, a grant was obtained for a further £4,500 and the finished Hall finally cost about £14,000 (around 1982 a further plot of land adjacent to the Hall was acquired from the Pullen family to provide additional car parking).

Two villagers, friends from schooldays, deserve a mention here. Cliff Howden and Ted Sparrow were insatiable fund raisers and in eleven years from 1964 raised more than £3,000 for Cancer Research and a further £1,600 towards the new Village Hall continuing their efforts after the hall was built to provide further equipment. Raising the money was achieved by arranging numerous social events attracting enthusiastic support from the villagers and people from the neighbouring countryside. In 1975, it was reported that on Easter Monday a major whist drive operating 65 tables was staged, with smaller ones held between Christmas and Easter, together with three Fives-and-Threes dominoes drives and fortnightly Bingo sessions, the caller on those occasions being Roy Everatt.

So it was that on Monday, Spring Bank Holiday, 28th May 1973, the Chairman of the Lindsey Village Hall Committee, Mr. Vincent G. Hudson, formally declared the new Village Hall open. All the village organisations had combined to provide a week of entertainments following the Grand Opening, with the Youth Club putting on an evening's variety show, the WI holding a coffee evening with various stalls, a fives-and-threes domino drive run by J. Sleight and A. Dawson, a dance, and a children's concert. The week concluded with a United Thanksgiving Service in the Hall with the Ashby Salvation Army Band providing the music.

The only hitch occurred at the very beginning of the festivities when a schoolboy spotted the sign over the door read "VILLIGE HALL". The sign was hastily covered with black plastic and the embarrassing mistake quickly rectified.

BUILDINGS IN THE VILLAGE

Although the village of South Kelsey has been in existence for more than a millennium almost all the houses date from the beginning of the nineteenth century onwards and only the ironstone tower of St. Mary's church now remains as evidence of its antiquity.

One curious feature of the older houses between the Methodist Chapel and St. Nicholas's churchyard is that many of them are built gable end on to the road with their main entrance on the south side of the house. This occurs elsewhere in the country and can be explained because the plot of land (the "burgage") given to each tenant was so narrow that the house was built gable end to the road so that it and its outbuildings could be extended down the plot and access could be made down the side of the buildings to the back of the land.

For the first couple of decades of the twentieth century there was very little building carried out. Houses of Kelsey bricks dating from the early nineteenth century were interspersed by at least thirty single storey mud and stud thatched cottages sitting on the edge of the roads leading out from the Church, but one by one every picturesque but decaying cottage was pulled down and replaced by more modern buildings.

In 1900, a small thatched cottage on the crossroads contained a shop run by the Bacon family but in 1912 Joseph Balderson bought it, pulled it down and built a new brick house the following year. Rather than share the public well a little further along the Waddingham Road, he sank his own well in the yard which was used until mains water came to the village. Past Church farm, built in 1819 of South Kelsey bricks, which incidentally also had its own well , there were two thatched cottages, plus two more on the other side of the road and another down the lane beside the church. These too were demolished and the Council built Nos 3 & 4 St. Mary's Gate during the war in 1943 and Nos 1 & 2 shortly after. Two pairs of Council houses opposite the Recreation Ground, known as Skipworth Ridge were built sometime between 1920-30.

As an aside, at that time West Lindsey Council only built and rented out houses exclusively to agricultural workers who were married and had at least one child – no-one else need apply!

Windy Ridge is one of the older houses in the village probably built in the early half of the nineteenth century since when it has been extended in almost every direction. It was originally surrounded by buildings and stockyards that belonged to Caistor Road farm and where they kept their working horses stabled. These buildings were eventually sold and the land used to build three modern bungalows although part of the old yard wall still stands at the rear of the plot. The land actually belonging to Windy Ridge was all on the other side of the road, consisting of land, farmyard and sheds, plus an orchard. When Horace Fosten moved to Windy Ridge in the 1930s he used the land for dairy farming while his father Samuel and mother Louisa ran a tailoring and dressmaking business from **Keptie House** near the crossroads. In the 1950s Windy Ridge was bought by Edmund Isle Pullen who had moved from **Moss Cottage** on the Thornton Road where the Pullens had lived since the 1880s. He was a joiner by trade and worked from his joiner's shop called Stack Yard in the orchard opposite the houses still visible behind Windy Forge. When he died in 1982, the orchard and stockyard were sold.

Windy Forge bungalow was built on the farmyard while **East and West Orchard** bungalows were built in the orchard where villagers can still remember as children scrumping for apples. The old cowshed standing on the side of the road was for a short time converted for use as a sub-post office and store, but closed in 1997. On the roadside in front of the orchard used to be one of the village wells which fed a horse trough. The paddock which stretched from the orchard right down on to the Thornton Road past the last houses became the property of Church Farm but very recently the bottom half has been sold for development and the top piece given to the village linking the Village Hall to the Recreation Ground.

The Schoolhouse (Grade II listed) and adjoining headmaster's house standing on the crossroads were rebuilt in 1906 on the site of the original buildings dating from the beginning of the 19th century and were in use until 1974 when the school finally closed, but have now been converted to private use.

A narrow drive between the houses in Brigg Road opposite the church leads to the **Rectory of St. Mary's.** Old photos show an attractive double fronted white walled house with a gothic window probably Victorian, set in pleasant gardens, but unfortunately it was destroyed during the last War. On Saturday, 30th October 1942, a plane from the local airfield at North Kelsey Moor flew low over the village and one wing clipped the east end of Caistor Road farm causing the plane to crash into the front of the Rectory. Sadly the airmen were killed, but luckily the

Rev. Ireland and his wife were in the back kitchen having breakfast and were unharmed, if somewhat shaken! A modern house was built in its place after the war, but the Rector now lives in North Kelsey since the parishes combined and the new house has passed into private hands. In the interim period, the rector and his family lived at a house in the village owned by the Church Commissioners and until recently the present owners were still paying a peppercorn rent to them.

Further along the Caistor Road stands the old **Sunday School** building built in 1863 which belonged to the tiny **United Methodist chapel** next to the Bull Inn. As late as the 1950s people can remember attending services at the chapel, warming themselves at the stove standing in the middle of the room but it closed in October 1967. It now forms part of a row of three cottages but the end wall still retains the tall arched window of the old chapel.

On the same side of the road stands **Old Farmhouse (formerly Caistor Road Farm)** whose land stretched around the back of the houses and pub into the Thornton Road with yards, farm buildings and a large barn. Again this land has now been sold as a development site for a number of new houses. As mentioned before, they kept their farm horses in stabling behind Windy Ridge, and an orchard and pigsties occupied the site of the last bungalow in the village on the south side of Caistor Road. The small cottage attached to the side of the farmhouse was known as Bell's Cottage.

Opposite on the north side of Caistor Road at the edge of the village stands **Sunshine Farmhouse.** This was originally a small cottage dating from the 18th century and was subsequently extended in all directions. It had a well in an outhouse at the back and the story goes that one day someone, unaware of its existence, fell through the flagstones into the well – fortunately she was rescued shaken but relatively unharmed. There are several very old outbuildings and the remains of a crewyard and it is thought the bricks were made from clay dug in the field behind the house and fired either on site or at the South Kelsey brickyard on the canal. In the early days there was also a slaughterhouse at the back where local beasts were taken and a door in the east end of the house gave access to a butcher's shop. The door and window were subsequently bricked up. The property and its land were all part of the South Kelsey Estate but in 1963, the widow of the owner, Mrs. Montefiore, conveyed most of the land to the Mercantile and General and General Reinsurance Co. Ltd and over the next ten to fifteen years, the Company sold off the individual farms and houses.

Between the farmhouse and the modern house, **Comfrey,** next door, is a small triangle of ground in which stands a rose tree planted in memory of his wife by Mr. Martin, who was the tenant of Sunshine Farm before it was sold off, and at his request carefully tended for many years by the present owner of Comfrey, Margaret Husband.   John Husband, who had built the house in 1960-1, had for some years been the captain of the South Kelsey Tennis Club and was also the dedicated leader of the Youth Club for 25 years.   A plaque to his memory can be seen in the Village Hall.

Thomas Harrison farmed at Hall Farm in the 1860s but later moved to Westfield Farm at North Kelsey Carr. His grandsons Harold and John (Jack) Harrison lodged with their married sister, Lily Bell, at **School Farm**, at that time a thatched house next to the Sunday school building on Caistor Road. Jack Harrison worked on School Farm in partnership with his brother-in-law, until he died, while Harold, the youngest of twelve children, went to work first for a Mr. Farrow, and then in the late 30s, at the Brigg Sugar factory. He served in the Royal Engineers during the War and then returned to work there for another 24 years. In the meantime, he had married and moved to North Kelsey. School Farm was finally pulled down and replaced by **Sunday School Bungalow** and some of the land used for more housing.

The Bull Inn, (Grade II Listed) was built sometime before the Enclosure Act in 1794 and until 1912 had a high thatched roof. Early photographs show that entrance used to be made through a doorway in the wall on the Caistor Road. In the nineteenth century it was the meeting place of two Friendly Societies - the Ancient Order of Foresters and The Druids. It also had its own brewery at one time, visible on an aerial photo, together with a row of stabling both of which were demolished in the latter half of the twentieth century.   For some time during the last century there was a small "chippy" on the roadside at the end of the stables.

Melrose House sitting back from Thornton Road was built sometime at the beginning of the twentieth century by a family of Dawsons on the site of their original cottage. It was later acquired by Raby and Hardy who farmed, among others, **Holm Hill Farm.** It was then bought by Peter Rhodes of Market Rasen and re-named Abbeville. It has since changed hands at least twice and is now called **Highfield.**

Opposite the Village Hall is a row of cottages, the first of which was the old **Post Office**, all dating from the early 1800s or before and extensively renovated and altered. The post office and grocery stores were run by Mrs. Edna Fieldson and her family from 1910 until it was closed sometime around 1960. Between it and the next property stood a thatched cottage, since demolished, called **Ramblers' Cottage** which belonged to a Miss Polly Cope.

Ivy Cottage, situated opposite, stands on one of two adjacent ancient village closes (described as St. Mary's Garth on one old map). Unlike the majority of the South Kelsey estate, the land and cottage appear to have been privately owned and were changing hands regularly for money without reference to the Lord of the Manor from as early as 1667. The property then was described as consisting of cottage, croft, garden and orchard and included part of a field on the marshy Carrs near Holm Hill. When its owner, Jane Harrison of Upton made application to the Land Enclosure Commissioners in 1794 she was allotted a new enclosure field on the south side of Waddingham Road (then known as Spittal Road) a few hundreds yards out of the village. Jane Harrison appears to have been a wealthy woman with several land holdings and on her death in 1813 she bequeathed it to her niece Susannah Storey and thereafter to Susannah's daughters, Mary Ann and Susannah Storey. At that time the land and cottage were rented to Thomas Green at an annual rent of £18. Daughter Susannah married Thomas Little and moved to his farm in Tring, Hertfordshire, and when she too died, her husband sold his wife's inheritance to Charles Green in November 1873 for the sum of £850.

Queensfield, the Council estate beyond these cottages, was built around Coronation year by a builder from Kirton.

After the Caistor Canal was closed a water mill was built at Mill Lock utilising the fall of water there and as early as 1856 David Taylor was listed as a corn miller. By 1892 Robert Howden had taken over as miller and baker and the business stayed in the Howden family until 1925. When the watermill became derelict an engine driven mill was installed at **Mill Farm** in the centre of the village together with an adjoining bakery. Walter James Howden born in 1883 left school at 11 and went to work in the mill. He also delivered bread, cakes and flour in a pony and trap all round the surrounding area until Mill Farm was sold to Mr. Oaks who continued to grind corn for cattlefeed until well after the end of World War II. The Bakery however was allowed to stand idle.

The water mill on the canal has now disappeared without trace but a photo of the building still exists. One of the original millstones lay forgotten in the hedgerow for many years until it was retrieved and placed in the garden of the aptly named bungalow "Millstone" on the Caistor Road.

In the meantime, Walter Howden had moved first to Manor Farm for a short time, then to North End Lane, and finally bought the 64 acre Dale Farm in 1928.

Mill Farm was taken over by Jabez Manders after he married Mr. Oak's daughter, Annie, and he grew sugar beet, potatoes and corn and bred Landrace cross Large White pigs. After 35 years the farmhouse and all the farm and milling equipment were sold off. The bakery building still exists at the back of Mill Farm, but its tall chimney visible in old photos was blown down in the 1937 whirlwind.

A narrow lane running down the side of Mill Farm and crossing the public footpath to the fields beyond used to give access for the parish almshouses, probably built around the beginning of the nineteenth century and occupied by village pensioners until after World War II. They were subsequently demolished.

Opposite Mill Farm, down a long drive lies Kelsey House Farm, now called **Kelsey Place**. It was built in the early 1800s, probably by Philip Skipworth of Moortown, the then Lord of the Manor, unusually of light coloured bricks from the Owersby brickyard. In the 1890s, the Birkett family was in residence and around the turn of the century a large extension of local red bricks was built on the side facing the entrance drive. This slightly taller structure then became the main entrance to the house and added a lot more accommodation. The house is surrounded by landscaped gardens with a large 2-storey granary building close to the house. The granary was used by the villagers, until the Village Hall was built, for dances and whist drives. The small lake situated at the back of the house was only excavated at the beginning of the 21st century. The old farm buildings down by the canal-side were known as Riverside Farm at one time and were connected to Gravel Pit Farm on the north side of the canal. The two houses either side of the entrance to Kelsey Place were once farm cottages.

After Mr. Birkett went bankrupt, sometime early in the 1900s the Fusseys moved into Kelsey House, followed by Joseph Barr and his family in 1925. His son, Charles Barr took over in 1939 and when he in turn built **Lindum House** in 1965 and moved there, his son Alan took over Kelsey House and farmed there until 2000. When Charles Barr died around 1983 Lindum House was sold and converted for a time into a Nursing Home.

Across the lane from the present cemetery, **White Cottage**, was built around 1760 and extended at the front around 1810 and at the back. It was built of mud and stud with a thatched roof originally and two sturdy beams held the walls together. These were said to have been ship's timbers taken from boats plying the Caistor Canal. The house was set in a half-acre market garden. One morning in 1990 Flora Hurst had just gone to the front gate to pick up her newspaper, when a tanker with a full load of diesel slipped on black ice and skidding across the road crashed into the front bedroom of the cottage where she and her husband would have been sleeping minutes before, and missing her standing at the gate by inches. The impact shattered one of the ancient oak beams running through the house and they had to sleep on the kitchen floor for several weeks while the bedroom was repaired.

On the opposite side of the road is **Grassmere Cottage**, built in Kelsey bricks around 1800. Closer inspection reveals that the house was designed to front the old road, now a public footpath. Starting off as a simple "two up two down", the house was extended on both sides and a porch added to the front elevation. The property also owned several fields on the other side of the old road together with two field cottages. In the garden lies a gravestone showing the imprint of ancient brasses of a lord and his lady possibly of the Ayscough family which must have come at some time from the graveyard of St. Nicholas church opposite.

A **Primitive Methodist chapel** was built in the grounds of Grassmere Cottage right on the edge of the road opposite the cemetery but pulled down sometime after 1945 to improve the corner of the road and the materials were used to build a carpenter's shop in North Kelsey for a Mr. Davy. A small **United Methodist** chapel was built beside The Bull (since converted to private use) and the third, **Wesleyan Methodist and its Schoolroom**, is still in active use on the corner opposite the old Forge Garage. It had been built in 1877 on the site of the old pinfold or cattle pound, where any stray animals were put to await collection by their owners.

The Chapel at Moortown was first built for the Wesleyans but later joined the Primitive Methodists. Around the chapel were five memorial stones commemorating the five ladies who each gave £5 towards the cost of the building. George Borman Skipworth, who was Lord of the Manor at the time, also gave £50. After it was closed in June 1970 the Chapel was dismantled and replaced by the white house called **The Lectern**. During the demolition a bottle was discovered hidden under one of the memorial stones containing a Queen Victoria Jubilee medal, a Methodist Recorder and a copy of that week's Market Rasen Mail.

All four Methodist chapels were listed in 1933. The separate **Sunday School** building still standing on the Caistor Road and which belonged to the United Methodist Chapel opposite, has also now been converted to a dwelling.

Prior to the building of the Wesleyan's chapel at Moortown, another chapel was built in the early 1800s, some 500 yards along the South Kelsey Road somewhere among the trees where each year there is a magnificent display of spring flowers. Looking at the old O.S. map of 1825 it can be seen that this chapel was already marked as disused, but it has been said that the building was also used as a blacksmith's shop before it finally disappeared.

Two thatched cottages standing by the road just past the Methodist chapel in South Kelsey were pulled down post World War II and many of the bricks used to build **Rose Cottage** further down. The small property tucked in beside it used to be a fish shop until some time after World War II. Behind the Chapel is a new development called Laurel Close. The land used to belong to **The Laurels** on the other side of the entrance, the owners also renting Mount Pleasant Farm in North End Lane, but when they moved to a new property on their old land they took the name of The Laurels, with them. The original house was called Willowdene for a short time but is now called **Eden House.**

In 1974, George Dannatt (born in 1909) closed his 150-year-old family joinery business His grandfather, Henry, a wheelwright, had taken over the joinery and undertaking business from the Kenningtons who had started work in South Kelsey in the late eighteenth century. Wheel making and wagon repairs were the stock in trade of the village joiner at that time. When the hurricane in 1937 flattened the brick-built workshop on the Brigg Road beside the Methodist Chapel, scattering his tools and equipment over a wide area, George thought himself lucky that he had chosen to go home for his dinner at that moment. The insurance company would not pay for repairs as it was regarded as "an Act of God", but everyone set to and helped each other to get back to business. The rebuilt workshop was finally demolished some years ago to widen the corner of the road. After 1974, Noel Hutchinson took over the joinery and decorating work in the village and helped in the building of many of the new bungalows and houses being erected at that time.

On the corner opposite the Methodist Chapel used to stand the village forge which since medieval times would always have constituted an essential part of village life. At the beginning of the 20th century, the blacksmith and farrier was Moses Staves but following a family argument his son did not follow him into the trade. Instead his son-in-law, George Blackburn took over on his death just after World War I, followed in turn by his son, Ron Blackburn, who converted the forge into an engineering works dealing mainly with agricultural machinery and car repairs. At one time petrol pumps stood in the front yard, and a small bicycle shop was also built on the front. Living in the house adjoining the works, he also farmed the land around it when it was known as **Forge Farm** The forge building was blown down in the 1937 whirlwind and rebuilt as the Forge Garage still to be seen with the house jutting out on the corner of the road.

For more than two centuries the Green family have lived in and around South Kelsey. As early as 1650 Henry Green and his wife Anne were known to have lived here while in 1706 his son, another Henry, is recorded as marrying Elizabeth Wickfall in the village, and when they died they were both buried here. In 1709 John Green, possibly his brother, sold Ivy Cottage and its land to Henry Monson but much later in 1873 it was bought back by Charles Green and has remained in the family ever since. In 1807, two of his grandsons, Robert and John, both in their sixties, were convicted at Brigg Petty Sessions for falsifying their loading accounts to the newly opened Caistor Canal, and were fined Twenty-seven Pounds as it was their second offence! The next generation saw Thomas marrying Susanna Clarke in 1805, and for a short time renting Ivy Cottage. His eldest son, Charles, was probably the Charles Green who had been farming at Winghale for a short time before selling up his stock in 1834 and later moving to **Manor Farm**. He married at the age of 42, Mary Wilkinson some ten years his junior and they had two sons, Richard and Thomas. Richard and his wife moved to Waddingham, but the younger son, Thomas, stayed on at Manor Farm. He and his wife, Susannah Grayson had twelve children in a neat sequence of girl/boy/girl/boy... Thomas owned several properties in the area, including housing and warehousing at Brandy Wharf for his coal merchant business, and gave four of his sons their own farms at Caenby, Thoresway, Waddingham and Glentham. Before he died in 1927 at Caenby, he had bought Manor Farm from the South Kelsey Estates. There are still Greens farming in the area today.

After more than half a century of occupation by the Green family, **Manor Farm** was eventually bought by Jack Foster in the 1930's. He was best remembered as keeping horses and ponies with which he competed at all the local shows and for allowing the village children to ride them "to give them exercise". He also owned one of the first private motor cars to be seen in the village. Manor Farm finally came into the possession of the Umpleby family who bought it in 1948 and now farm there.

After the death of the last male Ayscough heir, it is possible that Lady Mary Ayscough, Sir Edward's widow, may have continued to live at the old Tudor mansion for a while as it was she who was responsible for building the Free School in the village in 1712, but it is more likely that she moved back to Stallingborough and it is very unlikely that any of the Thornhagh family lived in South Kelsey after Letitia Ayscough, who had inherited the South Kelsey Manor in 1706, married Andrew Thornhagh as he had estates in Nottinghamshire. In 1771, Letitia's son, John Thornhagh Hewett mortgaged South Kelsey Hall to Robert Gunny of London. It was sold in 1780 and the old mansion finally demolished to be replaced around 1810 by the buildings now known as **Hall Farm**. However, for a large part of that century the farm was still known as South Kelsey Hall, occupied first by William Skipworth and then for a short time by Lionel Skipworth.

At the beginning of the twentieth century Walter Thomas Glew and his wife Grace are listed as living at Hall Farm, but earlier records show that Glews were living there as early as 1877. However, he and his family moved to Wittering some time before the outbreak of World War I. One son was killed during the war and the other was the first Lincolnshire airman (see story in Village Life).

Shortly after the War the farm was sold to William Francis Knapton who farmed there until he retired to North Kelsey when his brother Thomas Charles Knapton took over and farmed there until 1926. He then moved to **The Pines Farm** at Moortown and his son, Francis William Knapton, took over the 436 acre Hall Farm at the age of 23. He added another farm to his holding bringing the acreage up to over 600. He specialised first in Lincoln Red cattle and Lincoln Longwool sheep, but later turned to British Friesians. He loved horses and was a well-known breeder and exhibitor of Shire horses. He died in 1966 at the age of 63. He was succeeded by his son, Keith, who continued the running of the farm until recently when he and his wife retired to a bungalow on the Thornton Road and his son Andrew took over Hall Farm.

The latest addition to the village is the new **Hall Farm Park** opened in March 2006 which provides visitors with a café/tearoom, indoor and outdoor children's play areas and a collection of rare breed animals.

In 1905, Charles and Anne Fanthorpe and their two sons, Fred and Joseph, came from Killingholme and rented **Church Farm** which had been built in 1809 of South Kelsey bricks and stands at the crossroads opposite the church. Anne died shortly after in 1909. When he married, Fred and his wife Francis, moved to **Rose Cottage** near the Old Post Office, while his father and brother and his wife, Sarah, continued to live at Church Farm. Charles Fanthorpe died in 1925 aged 91 by which time the farm had been bought from the landowner and his two sons continued under the name of Fanthorpe Brothers until Fred died in 1945 aged 78 and Joseph was joined by John Parkinson. John Parkinson married Joseph's daughter, Gladys in 1945, and three years later Joseph died at the age of 70. (His wife, Sarah, died in 1963 at the good old age of 91). John Parkinson took over the farm and when he too died, his son, another John, continued to farm there.

The Parkinson family had been living in the parish for many years – in 1882 Jesse Parkinson, Skin Dealer, was living at Riverhead (Moortown), in 1892 Herbert Parkinson, Builder, and Joseph Parkinson, carpenter and farmer were also listed in the Kelly's Directory. There was also a family of Parkinsons farming the 100-acre **Corner Farm** at Moortown crossroads – the double-fronted white house standing on the Market Rasen road. It was here that John Parkinson had grown up before the family moved to Westholm Farm on the north side of the canal.

Corner Farm has not always been a farmhouse. In 1850 Mr.Skipworth built two public houses at Moortown to serve the men using the canal. The one on the south side of the cross roads, now Corner Farm, was known as "The Anchor", and the house still retains a cellar, but the name and location of the other one on the northern side is unknown. The pubs would not have been in use for long as the canal was closed down shortly after this date when the railway arrived, and the **Skipworth Arms** was built beside the railway line. The warehouse and offices on the canal basin were converted to private housing and known as **Riverhead** while the basin itself was filled in and built upon although not without some problems as the reclaimed land subsided and special foundations had to be constructed.

The properties on the north side of the Nettleton Road, used to be four cottages but each pair was converted into one house. The end one, known as **Letterbox Cottage** used to have a letter box let into the wall when the cottage was used as a post office.

In the Lincoln Rutland & Stamford Mercury of 1815 an advertisement appeared for a tenant for the new watermill built at Moortown by Mr. Philip Skipworth who had very recently acquired the South Kelsey estate and was to build Moortown House on the Brigg road for his family's occupation the following year.

The mill was situated about 50 yards from **Watermill Farm**, straddling a secondary loop of the Nettleton Beck It ran through very sandy soil and frequently silted up causing flooding higher up. There was a small mill pond feeding the mill race and the three storey building had a water powered pulley to take grain up to the top floor to feed the grindstones. It also powered a circular saw for cutting timber.

The first known tenants appear to have been the William H. Gibbons' family mentioned in the Trades Directories and the Church Registers in 1877, 1887 and 1907. Around 1916 the farm was acquired by Frederick Strawson of Thoresway, probably from Walter Boynton who had been Lord of the Manor around that time but who, because of financial difficulties, had been selling off some of his estate. Frederick Strawson did not live at the farm itself but kept a manager there. In 1933, William Would was listed as foreman in charge at the Mill. Frederick Strawson kept saddleback pigs and sheep and grew carrots used mainly to feed the pigs while the Mill was used to grind barley as feed for the animals. In 1936, Frederick's son, John, (who still lives at Croxby) remembers going over to Walesby to bring back a specialist carpenter, Mr. Porter, who fitted new teeth to the wooden cog wheel of the mill. John also remembers washing the carrots in the stream by rocking them in a sort of wooden cradle to get rid of the dirt before tipping them out. In the covered space over the mill race it was always cool and when an animal was slaughtered the carcase was hung there to keep it fresh.

In the 1940s, the Strawsons sold the farm to the Oliver Brothers, when the mill was still being used to grind animal feedstuff, and another villager remembers painting the mill during the 1960s. In the 1980s, Nickersons of Cherry Valley Farms bought the whole property and the mill was finally pulled down. Scarcely anything remains now of the mill, only a few bricks at the side of the ditch which was once the millstream.

After the disappearance of the post mill on Mill Road in the early nineteenth century, another notice appeared in the Lincoln Rutland & Stamford Mercury in December 1828 advertising the sale by private contract by the owner, Mr. Richard Nocton of the newly erected post corn mill, on the junction of North End Lane and Brigg Road. One could conjecture that the old mill had been dismantled and rebuilt in a more convenient location on the main road close to the newly opened canal. Although some of the older villagers will say they can point out the sites of both mills, the only signs are perhaps a slight mound in the earth.

Moortown House standing back from the Brigg/Market Rasen Road was built by Philip Skipworth in 1816 for his family's occupation after he acquired the ownership of the South Kelsey estates and remained the Skipworths' family home until the late 1890s.

The landscaped grounds were designed by Sir Joseph Paxton and contain a sundial dating from the early 19th century. There is a gatehouse at the entrance and cottages and outbuildings on the side of the old lane which used to lead to North End.

During World War I Moortown House was occupied by the Army and the soldiers would have helped in the harvesting of local crops, as they did at nearby Nettleton. In 1923, the house was occupied by one Harold John Smith, but from 1926, Charles F Stow, farmer, was living on the property, most probably in the farmhouse adjoining rather than in Moortown House itself, for the next ten years or so.

When Samuel Knapton bought the estate in 1938, the house was derelict. He contemplated knocking it down and rebuilding, but the fabric of the building was still good and his father-in-law who was a builder undertook the alterations. He first demolished the whole west wing containing some 17 rooms but which still left a substantial house and then renovated the rest of the building. During World War II the house was commandeered by the Army for a short time. An officer and his batman came each morning to take command of some soldiers who had returned from France and who were housed in the outbuildings. On three other occasions, families of airmen serving at the Nettleton Gap airfield were accommodated in the house for short periods. Samuel Knapton died in 1942, but his brother, Francis Henry Knapton continued to farm there until it was sold in 1950 by Mrs Ruby Knapton to a Mr.Sergeant. At that time the estate consisted of 545 acres of mixed farm land, Moortown House itself, two good sized detached houses, a pair of brick cottages and a Lodge cottage, together with substantial outbuildings, and boasted "a capital partridge shoot". In 1956, Moortown House again changed hands to its present ownership.

ST. MARY'S CHURCH

When any freshly cleared land was made available for cultivation and the newly settled population required the services of a priest, the Anglo-Saxons set up lesser "field churches", later referred to as chapels of ease or parochial churches. These were often provided by the principal owner of the newly cleared land on temporary licence and services held in a room or building on the landlord's homestead before providing a designated building. Such a licence for a chapel was granted to South Kelsey. It had no endowment and was served by a stipendiary priest employed by the landlord.

No mention of an actual church is made in the Domesday Book of 1084 so it can be assumed from the list of rectors that the first church to be built was that of St. Nicholas around 1190 whilst St. Mary's, referred to later as Keleseie Parva (or crossroad church) was built some time later around 1228. Although no trace remains, St. Nicholas was sited in the current graveyard at the other end of the main street.

The churches of St Mary's and St. Nicholas were probably built to serve two distinct communities and were treated as two separate parishes but as they did not expand much during the following centuries, it made economic sense to combine the congregations. The selection of a rector was for St. Nicholas – the lord of the manor, and for St. Mary's – the Crown. Thus around the same time as the land enclosures were taking place at the end of the eighteenth century, an official amalgamation of St. Nicholas and St. Mary's parishes was made and the choice of rector was divided alternately between the Crown and the Lord of the Manor.

Although a record exists of an Ann Fairfield being baptised at St. Nicholas Church on 3rd February 1788, by this time it must already have been falling into decay as part of its remains were used in 1795 in the rebuilding of St. Mary's. The St. Nicholas Rectory, together with its outbuildings had apparently been burnt down some years before this. Contemporary records describe it as having stabling, a large tithe barn and two buildings described as belfries, with land attached to the house and more land in the common fields. However, no evidence appears to exist as to where exactly it was built but presumably it was close by the church.

With the amalgamation of the two parishes it was also hoped to encourage the incumbent to reside in the village. As St. Nicholas church was in ruins and its rectory burned down some years earlier, the vicar of St. Nicholas, the Rev. Twigge, cousin of Francis Foljambe, who was also vicar of Tickhill, presumable went back to live there, while the rector of St. Mary's, the Rev. Bowra took up residence in St Mary's rectory.

St.Mary's church itself is a Grade II Listed building with the original embattled ironstone tower with pinnacles (now removed for safety reasons) and is thought to have been built around 1228, with a clock and a peal of three bells. The largest of these bells, and the earliest, dates from 1500. The founder was John of York and is inscribed in Latin – "In nominee Jesu Maria". It is 37" in diameter and weighs 9 cwts. The second largest dates from 1768 and is inscribed "Robert Cox, Churchwarden". It is 35" in diameter and weighs 7 cwts. The third's founder was Henry Oldfields and is inscribed "Jesus be our spid" (speed) and dates from 1620. It is 33" in diameter and weighs 6 cwts. The tenor bell was re-hung in 1900 and a new clapper fitted. The old clapper hangs on the wall of the tower but it is some years now since the peal of bells was rung since the timbers of the bell tower were deemed to be unsafe.

In 1482 there is a record of a bequest being made in the will of Elizabeth Chittok, widow of a London draper, for the upkeep of the sanctus bell at St. Mary's. The Church Wardens would have been responsible for providing the new ropes and bell frame and would have paid the clerk to ring the bell from early morning to curfew. The idea of the curfew bell was introduced by William the Conqueror who decreed that each day a bell should be rung at nightfall and citizens must go indoors and extinguish all fires (curfew = cour feu = cover fire) as a safety precaution.

In 1795 the main body of the church was rebuilt by William Porden with a decorated chancel and nave of four bays. The walls were plastered and wooden wainscoting fitted – now painted light blue. The stained glass east window was erected in 1853 as the gift of George Skipworth. Two side windows were added in the latter half of the nineteenth century and inscribed "To the glory of God and in loving memory of Frederica Mary Emily, only child of Frederick and Mary Brewster who died June 12th 1880 aged 19 years." No record of this family can be found in the Church Registers but the name of the rector at that time was Herbert Brewster.

In the same year, 1853, St. Mary's was thoroughly renovated under the direction of W. Butterfield, FSA, and a new organ from Forster & Andrews of Hull, was installed on 6th August 1853, at a cost of £77, the money having been raised by public subscription . For many years someone was paid to operate the organ pump but in the second half of the last century an electric blower was finally fitted, the gift of the vicar's wife in memory of her mother.

The next restoration work was carried out in 1889, under the direction of Mr. C. Hodgson Fowler, architect of Durham, the cost of £950 being paid for by the daughters of George Skipworth in memory of their parents. The church now provided 300 sittings. In recent years the church was re-roofed in 2000 and the porch in 2002.

The west window in the belfry tower is of special interest since it has a plaque beneath it bearing the following words:

"In memory of Louisa Blanche, the beloved wife of Cecil George Savile Foljambe of Cockglode and eldest daughter of Frederick John and Lady Fanny Howard. She died 7 October 1871 aged 29 and is laid with her second son in the vault of Scofton Notts. The above window is erected by her sorrowing husband. 1877".

(Note: Sadly, one of the panes on the actual window has been broken but the inscription appears to say approximately the same thing).

Cecil Foljambe was the great grandson of Francis Foljambe, who had sold the South Kelsey estates some 70 years previously.

Another very interesting plaque located in the belfry commemorates the gift of the recreation ground to the village. It reads:

"In gratitude to Almighty God for the kindness and love of Rosamund Frances Skipworth (born 21st November 1823 at Moortown House, died 30th August 1908), 2nd daughter of George & Amelia M Skipworth, her sisters Susan and Charlotte and 19 nephews and nieces have given 3-3/4 acres of land to the people of her native parish as a playground for their use forever. By love serve one another".

Within the north wall of the nave is a stone effigy of a knight in 13th century chain mail and cyclas (a long skirted surcoat) bearing a shield with the arms of Hansard at the time of Edward I. This may well represent Robert Hansard who distinguished himself in the Scottish Wars during Edward's reign (1271-1307). It is just possible to see the remains of the red and yellow paint with which it was originally decorated. The Hansards of Walworth Castle Co. Durham became the Lords of the Manor of South Kelsey in late fourteenth century and built the original moated and fortified manor house on the Thornton Road, now replaced by Hall Farm.

In the chancel are effigies in brass, formerly set into the floor, of a knight in full armour and a lady – Sir Richard Hansard, Sheriff of Lincoln in

1419 (died 1428) and his wife Joan who both lived at South Kelsey Hall. Although damaged these two brasses are listed on a National Register.

In 1966, St. Stephen's church on Guernsey offered a triptych to St. Mary's as a gift in return for covering the cost of insurance and packing. However, the Diocesan Board turned down the application for a facility to install it, saying it was too big for the church, so the gift was declined.

In 1968, a set of seven large 19th century paintings, thought to have come from St. Paul's Church Burton-on-Trent was offered to the rector of St. Mary's. One was placed by the altar, but as no-one liked it there it was placed with another to match on the west end of the nave. The remainder were presumably returned. It is possible that the large wooden plaque bearing the Royal Arms of George IV (reigned 1820-1830) came from the same source but its origin is not certain. A wooden chair dated 1690, of unknown origin, stands next to the altar. The heavy wooden lectern came from the defunct church at Kingerby in the 1950s, while the carved wooden bench by the north door, together with the interesting old iron wheeled coffin bier (previously donated by Fanny Skipworth), both came from the Chapel of Rest in St. Nicholas cemetery when it was dismantled. The wooden pews date from the nineteenth century.

Three fine 15th century candlesticks, made in Seville, were reputedly acquired by the Duke of Aloa whilst on a Spanish campaign, and finally purchased by Miss Fanny Skipworth for the Church.

Of particular interest is the handsomely carved wooden pulpit. This was made by the Rev. Charles H Brewster and hand carved by him using only a pocket knife. He had been given the living by George Skipworth in 1865 and served the parish as rector for 48 years, dying at the old Rectory in sight of his beloved church at the age of 82, although in the last year or so due to failing health his curate was carrying out most of his duties. His two daughters, Mary and Jenny were still living at the Rectory on his death. Jenny, who had sometimes helped in teaching the younger pupils at South Kelsey school, died unmarried in 1935 at the age of 65 whilst living at Scallows Hall, Binbrook, but she too is buried at South Kelsey. The Rev. Brewster was always very interested in the history of the village and its church and wrote South Kelsey Notes, as well as drawing a plan of South Kelsey Hall. He commissioned the Chapel at the cemetery in memory of his wife and they are both buried in St Mary's churchyard.

In an undated letter from the Rector (probably the Rev. Ireland) to a Miss Major at Lincoln, he offered to hand over two silver chalices dated 1569 and 1570, at that time housed in the Rectory safe, to the Church

Authorities there, since there was no need for them having two modern chalices in use. It is thought these are probably now kept in the Cathedral Museum.

In 1964, the retiring rector, Rev. A.H Hibbett gave the church an ewer for baptisms.

On the south wall of the church is a Sicilian marble slab, given by John Fox (possibly the farmer living at College Farm in 1933) bearing the names of the men of the parish who fell in the Great War 1914-18. Another smaller tablet with the names of those who gave their lives in World War II can also be seen on that wall.

Old photos show that in the early 1900s the churchyard wall was much higher than it is today. There was no gateway at the west end, and the east gate was surmounted by a wrought iron archway with a lantern, between two brick piers. Trees lined the boundary until they were blown down in the 1937 hurricane, to be replaced by the holly trees one sees today.

On the west side of the church, in the shadow of the huge sycamore tree that survived the 1937 whirlwind, an impressive stone tomb commemorates about a dozen members of the Skipworth family. This again is a Grade II Listed monument. Philip Skipworth of Aylesby bought the Manor lands of South Kelsey around 1800 and built Moortown House on the north-eastern boundary of his estates for his family's occupation. The family lived there throughout the nineteenth century.

The last burial in St. Mary's churchyard was that of the Rev. Richard Ireland and his wife, whose coffins were, due to lack of space, buried one on top of the other by the porch door.

The churchyard of the now vanished St. Nicholas church at the other end of the village street is now the current cemetery for the village. At the turn of the 19th century, the churchyard of St. Mary's was almost completely filled, so in 1901 the disused churchyard of St. Nicholas was drained to enable it to be used as a second village graveyard. It was estimated that it would provide sufficient unused ground for 150 years or so. However, due to the distance between the parish church of St. Mary's and the new graveyard, in 1906 permission was granted by the Diocese of Lincoln for the erection of a Mortuary Chapel for the sole use of those attending funerals. It was to be built under the direction of Mr. Hodgson Fowler at a cost of £275.15s.0d, which sum would be paid for by the Rev. Brewster who had commissioned the building in memory of his wife.

Unfortunately the chapel gradually fell into disrepair and in the 1980s the Manpower Commission gave the work of dismantling the building to a gang of unemployed men who used the bricks to rebuild the perimeter wall of St. Mary's and form a second access on the west end of the churchyard. Close by this gateway is a plaque let into the wall inscribed HCB & JB 1906 – probably the original dedication tablet from the mortuary chapel which commemorated the Rev. Brewster's wife. The site of the Chapel can be identified by the bramble covered mound in the corner. Much of the stone was taken away to be used in the building of the road bridge over the canal and as hardcore, but one intriguing gravestone survives in the garden of Grassmere Cottage. The slab used to contain brass inlays of a man and woman apparently dressed in Tudor costume, but no clue is left of their identity. It would be tempting to think it might be that of one of the Ayscoughs who were buried in South Kelsey.

One very interesting monument in the new cemetery is that to Aubrey Edmond Glew, 2nd Lieut. RFC, son of Walter and Grace Glew of Hall Farm, who was killed in France in the Battle of the Somme in 1916. This is one of only a handful of memorials in the country dedicated to a member of the Royal Flying Corps in World War I. There is also a cross commemorating Sidney Chappel of the RAF whose name appears along with Walter Henry Tutty RN. on the WWII plaque in the church.

At the present time, St. Mary's is the mother church to the combined parishes of Thornton-le-Moor, Holton-le-Moor, Kirkby-cum-Osgodby, North Kelsey, North Owersby and Usselby. In the past the patronage of the living was alternately in the gift of the Crown and the Lord of the Manor.

GLOSSARY OF TERMS

GARTH – an enclosure, yard, or garden

CLOSE – enclosed land or field.

EYES – high ground, dry island set in marshy ground

CARR – marshy ground used as pasturage during the dry season

TOFT – back yard of cottage (also a small grassy hedged-in field, a small grassy hill or the site of an old ruin)

CROFT – back garden and paddock

FURZE LEAS – rough moorland type ground

WARLOTT – meadow land

INGS – pasture

WARREN – managed land for breeding rabbits.

WAPENTAKE – sub-division of land for administration, similar to "hundreds" in other counties

FEUDAL SYSTEM – in 1086, all land in England "held of the king". All great "vassals" of the king were compelled to have a certain quota of knights, or horsemen, completely armed and to maintain them in the field for a period of 40 days. The King could thus raise 60,000 horsemen at any one time.

The King's barons granted out smaller manors to inferior persons to be held under them – such arrangement was termed "an honour". Each year the baron would summon "an honour court" at which all the freeholders of his manors were required to attend. These "free" tenants were obliged to serve on horseback and owed the baron their fealty and homage i.e. "knight's fee". The feudal system was abolished in the reign of Charles II

FEE – a grant of land for feudal service.

FIEFF – to grant possession of a fief or property in land.

FIEF – land held in fee, or on condition of military service.

KNIGHT'S FEE – a holding of land for which knight service was required (usually about 5 hides i.e. 5 x 120 acres)

VILLEIN – "unfree" tenant (husbandman in stage of vassalage) who held land – average 15-40 acres - in return for work on the Lord's demesne. Could not leave without Lord's permission.

SOC – The right of holding a local court (Also SOKE)

SOCAGE – tenure of lands by service fixed and determinate in quality.

SOKEMAN – a tenant by socage

BORDAR – cottager

STEWARD – Lord's chief representative of village, in his absence responsible for the control of the village answerable to the Lord if something went wrong.

REEVE – elected by and from villains, under the control of the Steward, responsible for ensuring the serfs completed their labour service for their Lord, in conjunction with the Bailiff.

MESSOR – village official responsible for the work done in the fields.

WOODWARD – responsible for the woodlands.

HAYWARD – responsible for the proper upkeep of meadows and hayfields.

AFFEEROR – responsible for ensuring payment of fines imposed by Manor Court.

ALE CONNOR – responsible for controlling sale of village ale and only by those granted a licence by Manor Court.

PINDER – responsible for rounding up stray animals and putting them in a pinfold.

BEADLE – responsible for maintaining law and order in a village.

GARTHMAN – a man in charge of feeding stock cattle i.e. those to be fattened up for slaughter.

HUCKSTER – a retailer of small wares, a pedlar or hawker

LENGTHSMAN – road sweeper

GAD – a measurement of 2 roods, 2 perches and a half. (Gad, in Lincolnshire was a 6 to 7 feet wide strip division in a field)

PERCH – measurement of 20 feet.

ACRE – 40 perches in length x 4 perches in breadth.

BURAGE – strip of land granted to villager within the village

BOVATE – as much as a pair of oxen can plough in a year, usually about 15 acres (also known as OXGANG), normally up to an eighth of a Carucate.

CARUCATE – hide or plough-land – that is as much land as could be tilled every year by a great plough pulled by 8 oxen – average 120 acres, but amount could vary according to the superiority of the household.

BEASTGATE or cowgate – setting land aside to pasture a cow or the right to pasture a cow on common land.

BEREWICK – manors within manors.

MERCHET – or Maiden's rent – payment to the Lord of the Manor upon the marriage of a vassal's daughter, in lieu of his right to the virgin bridge ("droit de seigneiur").

LABOUR SERVICE – the work a tenant was expected to do for the Lord on his land.

HERIOT – the giving of one's best animal or chattel to the Lord on death and inheritance of land.

TALLAGE – tax paid to Lord each year by serfs.

TOLL TAX – tax paid to Lord when an animal was sold by its owner.

BOON WORK – extra days worked by villagers for Lord at busy times, harvest, ploughing, etc.

WEEK WORK – days of week working for Lord.

TUN – Saxon term for collection of family huts. Each family was given sufficient land for its support i.e. a carucate, plough-land or hide.

VILL – Saxon term for collection of huts within a stockade or similar defence – a unit for purposes of law and taxation.,

DEMESNE – the manor house and enclosed fields, or home farm, owned by the lord and cultivated with the aid of his tenants and servants.

BLACK DEATH – bubonic plague which swept through the country around 1349 and wiped out one-third of the population.

MURAGE – a "tax" for the fortification of a town wall

SCUTAGE – a "tax" for self-defence.

PONTAGE – a "tax" for bridge repairs.

INDEX

D

I

Immingham Docks, *65*
Indoor Bowls Group, *100*
Industrial Revolution, *89*
Ireland, *29, 33, 34*
Ireland, Rev., *104, 110, 124, 125*
Iron-ore, *68*
Ivy Cottage, *112, 116*

J

James II, *32*
Jarvis Plantation, *99*
Jenison, *29* Jessop,
61
John de Croquet, *12*
John of York, *122*
Johnston, *5* Joiner,
94, 109, 115
Joinery, *96, 115*

K

Katherine of Aragon, 27
Kay, *52*
Keelby, *45*
Kelly's Directory, 118
Kelsey Beck, 19
Kelsey Feast, 71
Kelsey House, 42, 95, 96, 106, 113
Kelsey House farm, 95, 106
Kelsey House granary, 96
Kelsey Place, 113
Kelsey St. Mary, 51
Kelsey Wives Group, 100
Kelsey Woods, 47
Kenningtons, 115
Kentish Rebellion, 26
Keptie House, 95, 109
Kettleby, 27, 43

King, *31*
King Harold, *23*
Kingerby, *124*
Kirkby, *95, 99*
Kirkby Shop, *95*
Kirkby-cum-Osgodby, *126*
Kirton in Lindsey, *28, 99, 103, 112*
Knapton, *117, 120*
Knight, *10, 23, 25, 27, 28, 123, 127, 128*
Koo Jam, *97*
Kyme, *46*

L

Lady Day, *70*
Lake, *113*
Lampreys, *18*
Land Enclosures Act of 1796, *15*
Latter Examination, The (1547), *48*
Laurels, The, *115*
Lawrence, *87*
Lea Hall, *42*
Lectern, The, *114*
Leeds, *62, 80, 97*
Legbourne, *37*
Legion of Volunteers, *35, 89*
Legsby Road, *93*
Leicesters, *35*
Lengthsman, *94*
Letterbox Cottage, *118*
Lighthouse, *32*
Lighting, *96*
Lincoln, *5, 10, 22, 28, 30, 37, 44, 46, 47,*
    49, 55, 56, 64, 65, 66, 67, 68, 82, 88,
    117, 118, 119, 124, 125
Lincoln Reds, *55*
Lincolnshire Chronicle, *74, 91*
Lincolnshire County Council, *95*
Lincolnshire Life, *93*
Lincolnshire Long Wool, *21*
Lincolnshire Rising, *28, 43, 44, 46*
Lincolnshire Yeomanry, *94*
Lindsey, *9*
Lindsey Battalion, *98*
Lindsey Village Hall, *107*

N

Nature Reserve, *99*
Navigation Lane, *61*
Nettleton, *10, 20, 21, 57, 60, 64, 68, 70, 77, 120*
Nettleton Beck, *60, 118*
Nettleton Bottom, *68*
Nettleton Feast, *71*
Nettleton Gap Airfield, *120*
Nettleton Moor, *68*
Nettleton Road, *20, 60, 64, 118* Nettleton Top, *68*
Neville, *25*
New River Ancholme, *59*
Newgate, *47*
Nickerson, *98*
Nickersons, *119*
Nocton, *119*
Non-Conformist, *84, 85*
Nor Pale, *9*
Normanby-le-Wold, *77*
North End, *20, 56, 57, 95, 113, 115, 119, 120*
North End Lane, *56, 95, 113, 115, 119*
North End Road, *20*
North Kelsey, *37, 42, 51, 56, 60, 66, 77, 88, 96, 104, 109, 111, 114, 117, 126*
North Owersby, *80*
North Willingham, *32*
Norton Disney, *45*
Nun Cotham, *45*
Nunnery Farm, *13*
Nursing Home, *113*
Nuts, *18, 93*
Nutthall Manor, *27, 32, 45*
Nutthall, *27, 28*

O

Oaks, *112*
October Feast (1866), *87*
Old Bakery, *66, 94*
Old Farmhouse, *110*
Old Tudor Hall, *11*

Oldest British Built Aeroplane, *94*
Oldfields, *122*
Oliver Brothers, *119*
Olney, *5*
Osberton, *32, 34*
Osgodby Hospital, *96*
Osland, *33*
Overseers of the Poor, *58*
Owersby, *13, 80, 113, 126*
Ownby, *98*
Oxford, *37, 84*
Oxford Street, Cambridge, 49

P

Padley, *5*
Pag Rag Day, *70*
Parish Council, *79, 102, 104, 106*
Parish Register, *22*
Parker, *67, 98*
Parkinson, *103, 104, 118* Parliamentarians, *30*
paupers, *75, 77*
Paxton, *120*
petrol filling station, *99*
Pickworth, *37*
Pig Club, *97*
Pigeon, *18*
Pigeon pie, *93*
Pigs, *18, 21, 64, 72, 90, 93, 97, 98, 113, 119*
Pigs, *90*
Pilgrimage of Grace, *28, 44*
Plumber, *93*
Pony and trap, *95, 112*
Poor Laws, *75, 76, 78, 80*
Poor Relief, *73, 75, 76, 77*
Pope Celestine III, *19*
Porden, *122*
Pormon, *43*
Post Office, *66, 99, 109, 111, 117 118*
Potato Setting, *87*
Poverty Bridge, *57*
Praxis Films Ltd, *99*
Prince Arthur, *27*
Prince Edward, *46*

White's Directory, *91*
Whitehead, *77*
Wickham Bishop, *38*
Wilby, *86*
Wilkinson, *41, 116*
William Count of Mortain, *12*
William I, *8*
William the Conqueror, *8, 12, 23, 122*
Willingham Hall, *65*
Willowdene, *115*
Windy Forge, *66, 109*
Windy Ridge, *109, 110*
Wingal Priory, *28*
Wingale, *13, 22, 30, 33, 57*
Wingall, *12*
Winghale, *5, 11, 12, 13, 14, 22, 59, 116*
Winghale Priory, *11, 12, 59*
Wingle, *12, 37, 54, 56, 57, 58, 59*
Wittering, *93, 94, 117*
Wittering Farm, *94*
Wolds, *7, 17, 18, 21, 22, 32, 35, 56, 60, 62, 104*
Women's Institute, WI, *100, 107*
Workhouse, *68, 74, 76, 77, 78, 80, 82, 90*

World War I, *94, 115, 117, 120, 126*
World War II, *83, 85, 96, 98, 112, 113, 115, 120, 125*
Worsley, *34*
Would, William, *119*
Wragby, *22, 50, 55*
Wrangle, *46*
Wray, *31*
Wright, *103*
Wriothesley, *47*
Wrottesley, *27, 45*

Y

Yorkshire Television, *100*
Youth Club, *100, 107, 111*

Z

Zeppelins, *94*

SOUTH KELSEY - NOTES

Lightning Source UK Ltd.
Milton Keynes UK
UKOW05f1458030117
291276UK00001B/231/P